I0751138

JUDOUS CONFESSIONS

ANDREW CONWAY-HYDE / B. JUDOUS

The authorship of the *Confessions of a Mr B. Judous and Epistles of a Jaded Muse* is, as with much of the material contained within, not entirely stable. The book is formally attributed to Andrew Lèon Conway-Hyde, Director at London Fine Art Gallery Ltd, where he has been associated (in various capacities) with curation, pedagogical consultancy, and the occasional structuring of critical frameworks for emerging artists. His published writings have previously appeared in institutional catalogues, internal teaching documents, and, on one documented occasion, a margin note later mistaken for an exhibition statement. Less formally, several of the letters within this volume circulate under the name **B. Judous**, a figure variously described as a senior academic, a pedagogical construct, or an administrative fiction generated to accommodate certain necessary tonal excesses within the University of Creative Studies. Attempts to verify whether Conway-Hyde and Judous are separate individuals have produced inconclusive results. Staff records from overlapping periods contain both names, though never in the same handwriting, and never with fully compatible signatures. Some archival copies list Conway-Hyde as "external reader"; others list Judous as "internal function." No document definitively resolves the distinction between these terms. It is therefore simplest to say this: One name appears in the institutional record. The other appears in the correspondence. Neither appears to contradict the existence of the other in any administratively actionable way. Recent cataloguing updates at London Fine Art Gallery Ltd still attribute editorial oversight to Andrew Lèon Conway-Hyde. However, annotated drafts recovered from earlier proofs suggest that sections of the Preface, as well as several marginal commentaries in the later letters, may have been written in a voice that predates that attribution. Whether this constitutes collaboration, succession, or misrecognition remains unresolved. Readers are advised not to treat this ambiguity as a puzzle to be solved. It is, more accurately, a condition under which the text continues to function.

First published in Great Britain in 2026
by London Fine Art Gallery Ltd.

A catalogue record for this book is available from the British Library.

Book and cover design by Andrew Léon Conway-Hyde

ISBN: 978-1-0685723-1-9

First Edition: 1st May 2026

Art is often a reflection of the artist's emotional state. As emotions shift, so too can the creative process. An artist may begin with a specific intention but find themselves led in a different direction based on their feelings at the moment.

Andrew Lèon Conway-Hyde

PREFACE

I have no intention of explaining how this correspondence, which I now present to you, came into my possession–whether by accident, indiscretion, or through that particular combination of curiosity and circumstance to which the art student is rarely immune. It is sufficient to say that no great effort was required on my part; indeed, one might suggest that such materials possess an inclination to reveal themselves to those who believe themselves prepared to interpret them. You may, if you wish, speculate as to the precise conditions under which these letters were obtained, though I would caution against allowing such speculation to displace the more substantive matter at hand. The question of how they arrived here is, ultimately, less significant than the question of what you are able–or willing–to make of them. There are, I think, two equal and opposite errors into which the academic world–and, by extension, the art student–can easily fall. The first is to underestimate one's own potential, adopting a posture of hesitation that inhibits meaningful development and renders even modest progress improbable. The second, perhaps more insidious, is to overestimate the significance of one's initial ideas, mistaking the intensity of ambition for the presence of originality, and conviction for clarity. It would be reductive to suggest that either position is wholly incorrect. Each contains, in its own way, a partial truth. What they share, however, is an incompleteness–an inability to sustain itself when exposed to the extended demands of practice over time. Gallery owners, who encounter such tendencies with predictable regularity, tend to observe them with a degree of measured detachment, their familiarity producing neither surprise nor particular urgency. For the student, however, these conditions rarely present themselves so neutrally. They are experienced as immediate, personal, and frequently decisive. The reflections contained within these letters may assist in negotiating this tension–but only insofar as they are approached with a willingness to question, rather than confirm, one's existing assumptions. They do not resolve the difficulty. They do not remove it. At best, they render it more visible, and therefore more difficult to ignore. It is also necessary to acknowledge that the figure of the gallery owner, as it appears within this correspondence, should not be regarded as entirely reliable. There is, perhaps inevitably, an element of performance involved–an inclination not merely to observe, but to shape perception. Even when adopting the tone of retrospective insight, the voice you encounter here is not exempt from distortion, nor from the subtle satisfactions of its own authority. I have made no attempt to identify the students described within these pages with any degree of specificity. The figures of *Eager Beatrice* and *Self-Doubting Simon*, among others, should be understood as conceptual approximations rather than definitive portraits. They are not individuals so much as positions–configurations of behaviour, assumption, and response that recur with sufficient frequency to acquire the appearance of familiarity. You may, at times, recognise aspects of your own position within them. This is neither accidental nor especially revealing. It would, however, be unwise to assume too direct a correspondence. The student, after all, is rarely as coherent to themselves as they might initially suppose–and even less so when observed. A further point of clarification concerns the organisation–or lack thereof–of these letters. No sustained effort has been made to impose a stable chronology upon them. Certain entries appear to precede the more demanding phases of study; others emerge from positions of greater familiarity, or even fatigue. This inconsistency is not incidental. It reflects the irregular manner in which time is experienced within the context of artistic education: as something alternately abundant and insufficient, structured and elusive, measurable and yet persistently resistant to measurement. External events–shifts in artistic discourse, institutional priorities, or developments within the broader social landscape–are registered only intermittently, and frequently subordinated to the more immediate concerns of making, reflecting, and attempting, not always successfully, to understand one's own work. Thus, I offer *Judous Confessions* not as a guide, nor as an argument in any definitive sense, but as a framework within which certain recurring difficulties might be examined without the expectation of resolution. It is, at best, a partial account –one that may illuminate, but just as easily obscure, depending on the disposition of its reader. What you take from it will depend, to a considerable extent, on what you are prepared to question in your own practice and, perhaps more importantly, on what you are not.

ANDREW LÉON CONWAY-HYDE

1

Dear Mr Jaded Muse,

Welcome again to our aged university. I trust you will settle in with the appropriate mixture of optimism and resignation. Both are necessary here, though neither is officially acknowledged in our documentation, which prefers the language of "opportunity" to that of endurance. You will find, in time, that the institution runs not on policy but on atmosphere–a condition maintained with great care and almost no accountability. The students, with admirable confidence, insist on misunderstanding this distinction, treating atmosphere as either incidental or, more curiously, as something they themselves produce. It is a forgivable confusion. After all, one must begin somewhere. I offer, therefore, some preliminary observations regarding our first-year fine art students, who have now entered what is being described–somewhat ceremonially–as a new era of Art and creative thinking. The phrase, as you will already suspect, is administrative fiction. Yet like all effective fictions, it does not remain inert. It circulates. It is repeated. It becomes, in time, indistinguishable from the conditions it was meant merely to describe. Students do not question its accuracy; they inhabit it. And it is always in the earliest phase of any newly declared artistic condition that a particular misunderstanding begins to take hold. Students, almost without exception, begin to mistake possession for participation. This error does not present itself crudely. It arrives dressed in sincerity, supported by language that appears, at first glance, entirely reasonable.

They speak of their experiences, their ideas, their processes–not incorrectly, but with a subtle inflexion of ownership that transforms occurrence into property. One observes this not as novelty, but as recurrence–predictable as the annual conviction, each winter, that one has always understood darkness, melancholy, and the cold. They do not encounter experience; they absorb it rhetorically, and then claim authorship. Thus emerges the first error: The student's belief that experience is something they own rather than something that occurs to them.

Fert nos vita, non ferimus vitam. (Life carries us; we do not carry life.)

You will hear them speak of "their practice" with the tone of a landlord describing inherited property–something to be managed, expanded, occasionally renovated, but never fundamentally questioned. It rarely occurs to them that practice, like weather, may proceed perfectly well without their consent, and may even improve in their absence.

This leads, naturally, to several interpretive positions, each of which deserves–at least briefly–our consideration. The **biographical position** suggests that students emphasise ownership because they are encouraged to locate meaning within personal experience. This is, in principle, sound. It produces work that is legible, emotionally accessible, and institutionally commendable. Its strength lies in its clarity. Its weakness, however, is that it quietly converts experience into material–something to be shaped, presented, and, crucially, possessed. The **institutional position** offers a different explanation. It argues that the language of ownership is not a misunderstanding but a requirement. Students must speak of "their work," "their voice," "their development," because assessment demands identifiable authorship. The strength of this position is its realism. The weakness is that it cannot distinguish between administrative necessity and ontological truth. The **psychological position**, often favoured by those with an interest in developmental frameworks, proposes that ownership is a necessary illusion–an early stage through which students must pass before arriving at a more complex understanding. Its strength lies in its patience. Its weakness lies in its optimism. Each of these positions explains something. None explains enough. The difficulty, as I suspect you already perceive, is structural. The student does not simply misunderstand ownership–they require it in order to stabilise themselves within a system that is, by design, unstable. Time, experience, and practice are not presented to them as indifferent conditions, but as resources to be managed. They are told, repeatedly, to "use their time," to "develop their practice," to "own their voice." It would be surprising if they did anything else. And so the second error emerges, closely related and perhaps more pernicious: They speak, with a seriousness that would be admirable in a less deluded context, of "their time," as though time were a possession rather than an atmosphere through which they are temporarily permitted to move.

De tempore suo loquuntur quasi de re ficta. (They speak of their time as though it were a fictional object.)

I have never been entirely certain what metaphysical arrangement permits such ownership, but they assert it with the confidence of those who have never been asked to account for it. Time, in their formulation, behaves very much like studio space: expandable, reclaimable, and–most importantly–interrupted only by external malice. You will notice that interruption is always attributed outward. No student has ever reported being interrupted by their own indecision, though it is the most frequent culprit. Allow me a brief pedagogical aside, offered not for implementation but for your private amusement: students exhibit approximately a 42% increase in perceived oppression when informed that deadlines are not symbolic constructs but administrative necessities. The remaining percentage typically requests clarification in writing, preferably after the deadline has passed. There is, incidentally, a curious relationship between colour choice and temporal delusion. Students who insist that time is "fluid" tend also to overuse blue–particularly the sort that promises depth without ever committing to it. I advise you to treat this not as coincidence but as a diagnostic indicator.

Nihil hic fortuitum. (Nothing here is accidental.)

Let us consider a recent case. A student arrives three days late to a critique, presenting a large canvas dominated by unresolved gradients and accompanied by a reflective statement in which time is described as "expansive," "non-linear," and "resistant to containment." The work is unfinished. The explanation is not. When asked about the delay, the student does not apologise but reframes: the lateness becomes "alignment with process," the incompletion becomes "refusal of closure," and the absence of resolution becomes "an intentional destabilisation of expectation." It is, one must admit, elegantly constructed. And yet, something persists beneath the language. The true difficulty is not that they misunderstand time, but that they aestheticise misunderstanding. Error, when named plainly, might be corrected; but when framed as intention, it becomes remarkably durable. One grows weary–not of failure–but of translating negligence into philosophy.

Querela fit ars ubi ars deficit. (Complaint becomes art where art fails.)

And here we arrive at the necessary inversion. It would be tempting–dangerously so–to correct the student directly. To explain that time is not theirs, that experience is not owned, that practice is not property. But such clarity would produce resistance. Students defend ownership not because it is correct, but because it is stabilising. We must therefore cultivate a more precise illusion: That time is theirs–but only in a conditional sense. Let them wake each morning as proprietors of twenty-four hours, while quietly ensuring that the University retains the right to reclassify those hours without notice. The effect, though subtle, produces in them a useful condition of interpretive instability–neither fully autonomous nor entirely constrained. You will find that nothing provokes a student more reliably than the discovery that the institution does not recognise their internal narrative as legally binding. A second observation, drawn from recent submissions: students are 37% more likely to include the phrase “time felt different” in reflective writing following missed deadlines. This is not, as some of our more optimistic colleagues suggest, a sign of insight.

Signum intellegentiae: semper suspectum. (A sign of understanding: always suspect.)

It is, rather, a sign of narrative adaptation–an attempt to convert consequence into atmosphere. You may also observe that scale behaves similarly. Students who lose track of time often increase the size of their canvases, as though duration might be compensated for by surface area. It never is. Large works do not indicate ambition; they merely render hesitation visible. What, then, is to be done? Nothing, directly. Avoid correction. Avoid clarification. Allow the misunderstanding to persist, but guide its consequences. It is always more productive that the student feels wrong than understands why. For there is, beneath all of this, a distinction which must be preserved, though never fully explained: They believe they are interrupted. We understand they are merely situated. They imagine themselves the centre of temporal experience. We regard them as one of its more vocal inhabitants. And this distinction–though rarely articulated–governs everything. For now, it is sufficient that they continue to believe they are managing their time, rather than being carried along by it.

Non possident tempus, sed ab eo possidentur. (They do not possess time, but are possessed by it.)

With measured regard,

B. Judous

2

Dear Mr Jaded Muse,

You report, with what I take to be a mixture of concern and administrative fatigue, that the students are "struggling" under the demands of this newly proclaimed era of Art and creative thinking. I find the observation both accurate and, in a rather technical sense, irrelevant. Struggle, in their case, is not an interruption of artistic development but its primary medium. It is not a deviation from process; it *is* the process, though one must be careful never to state this too plainly. Without struggle, they would be left alone with their actual abilities, which would be far more alarming–for them, certainly, and for us by extension. It is far better that they wrestle with difficulty than arrive prematurely at clarity. Clarity, in the first year, is almost always a form of concealment. Students who appear "clear" at this stage are rarely so. They have merely located a stable arrangement of language through which uncertainty can pass unnoticed. What appears resolved is often only well-disguised hesitation. This, then, is the first misreading: That struggle is a problem to be resolved, rather than a condition to be inhabited. It is, I concede, an understandable belief. Difficulty presents itself with such immediacy that one naturally assumes it requires removal. Yet in the context of artistic formation, removal is precisely what must be resisted. From this misreading emerge several positions, each persuasive in its own limited way. The **pedagogical position** suggests that struggle indicates a failure of instruction–that students are confused because they have not been adequately guided. Its strength lies in its compassion. Its weakness lies in its assumption that clarity can be transferred rather than constructed. The **psychological position** frames struggle as a developmental stage–necessary, but temporary. Students must pass through uncertainty in order to reach confidence. This is comforting, particularly to those tasked with monitoring progress. Its weakness, however, is that it imagines an endpoint at which struggle ceases, rather than recognising it as a recurring condition. The **biographical position**–favoured by the students themselves–interprets struggle as personal adversity. Difficulty becomes identity. One is not working through a problem; one *is* a problem in motion. Its strength lies in its intensity. Its weakness lies in its tendency to aestheticise discomfort before understanding it. Each position explains the presence of struggle. None explains its function. The matter, as ever, is structural. Struggle persists not because students are incapable, nor because instruction is insufficient, but because the system requires a continuous misalignment between expectation and capacity. If expectations were perfectly calibrated to ability, no work would occur. It is the gap–the irritation, the friction, the mild but persistent failure–that produces movement. Struggle, therefore, is not an error in the system. It is its organising principle.

Experientia accidit, non acquiritur. (Experience happens; it is not acquired.)

You will have noticed, for example, that their relationship to colour is still largely anecdotal. At present, they do not know where yellow comes from and relate it more readily to a late night out than to any perceptual or physiological condition. It may amuse you–though you must never show it–that yellow is not "out there" in the world at all, but occurs when light activates the red and green receptors simultaneously, leaving the blue conspicuously silent. The colour is therefore not a property, but an event–an agreement between eye and stimulus. Yet they will insist, with great sincerity, that they are "working with yellow," as though it were a cooperative material rather than a perceptual incident. This tendency–to treat experience as possession–returns here in miniature. They do not encounter colour; they claim it. And when that claim fails–when the work does not cohere, when the outcome resists intention–struggle is immediately reinterpreted. Not as limitation, but as injury. Here we encounter the second misreading: That inconvenience is evidence of injustice. A delayed critique becomes neglect; a correction becomes hostility; a lack of praise becomes institutional violence. One almost admires the efficiency of the transformation, though admiration must be carefully rationed, as it is frequently mistaken for endorsement. Allow me a brief diagnostic observation, offered in confidence: students are approximately 44% more likely to describe themselves as "misunderstood" within twenty-four hours of receiving feedback that contains more than three sentences. The percentage rises sharply if the feedback includes punctuation–particularly the semicolon, which they regard as a personal attack. What we are witnessing, therefore, is not resistance to instruction but the rapid development of a secondary practice: The production of explanatory frameworks for why the primary work could not succeed.

Querela fit ars ubi ars deficit. (Complaint becomes art where art fails.)

They no longer merely produce work; they produce interpretations of its failure, often with greater fluency than the work itself. These interpretations are not incidental. They are structured, rehearsed, and–most importantly–shared. For nothing produces such immediate coherence among students as the discovery that their expectations have not been met. Disappointment, in this context, is contagious. There is a peculiar synchronisation in their dissatisfaction, as though disappointment itself were a shared curriculum outcome. One student begins to feel overlooked, and within hours, an entire cohort begins to feel structurally oppressed by the concept of attention.

Attentionis structura eos opprimit, sed libertatem eam appellant. (The structure of attention oppresses them, but they call it freedom.)

It is worth retaining a principle that has served me reliably over the last fifty years: students do not require shared experience in order to develop shared grievance; they require only shared vocabulary. Once terms such as "validation," "space," and "voice" enter circulation, reality becomes negotiable in precisely the wrong direction. There is, incidentally, a visual analogue to this phenomenon. Students who feel insufficiently "seen" tend to increase contrast in their work–sharper blacks, louder whites–as though visibility could be engineered through tonal aggression. It cannot. One merely produces a louder confusion.

Lingua visualis communis—sed vix intellecta. (A shared visual language—yet scarcely understood.)

And yet—here we must proceed carefully—it would be a mistake to eliminate complaint entirely. This is where the inversion becomes necessary. Complaint, though frequently misguided, performs a crucial function. It converts passive discomfort into active articulation. A student who complains is, at the very least, engaged. The danger lies not in complaint itself, but in its interpretation. A complaint left unchecked becomes stagnation. A complaint properly structured becomes ambition. The distinction is subtle but critical. Another observation: students who are given explicit permission to express dissatisfaction tend to increase dissatisfaction output by approximately 61%, with a corresponding 23% decrease in clarity regarding its origin. This is entirely predictable. If one encourages emotional production, one should not be surprised when form follows volume rather than meaning. The most effective complaints are those that begin as private discomforts and end as public philosophies. A student who once felt ignored will soon develop a theory of systemic invisibility; a student who once disliked critique will draft, with alarming speed, an informal manifesto on oppressive evaluation structures. The University, for its part, remains blissfully unaware that it is being continuously reinterpreted by those it is simultaneously assessing. And so, we arrive at the necessary pedagogical posture. Do not remove their sense of injury. Refine its direction. Let them believe they are reacting to external conditions, while quietly ensuring they are, in fact, reacting to their own interpretive habits. A student who believes they are oppressed will work tirelessly to define the structure of that oppression; a student who understands nothing is wrong will simply withdraw, or worse, become content.

Ubi cecideris, ibi dormias. (Where you fall, there sleep.)

We are not, after all, in the business of comfort–but of sustained, productive discomfort, carefully misrecognised. Thus, the final distinction must be preserved: They believe struggle is imposed upon them. We understand it is the condition through which they are formed. They seek resolution. We maintain the tension that makes resolution possible. And it is within this tension–misread, resisted, and repeatedly reframed–that all useful work occurs.

With structured regard,

B. Judous

3

Dear Mr Jaded Muse,

It appears your students are, in your understated phrasing, "tired." I find this encouraging. Fatigue, properly understood, is one of the few remaining reliable instruments in contemporary artistic education–though it is almost never recognised as such by those subjected to it, nor by those tasked with administering it. The University, as you will have noticed, prefers to categorise fatigue as either a scheduling error or a welfare concern, both of which can be addressed with sufficient paperwork. The possibility that fatigue might be pedagogically useful is, for reasons both ethical and bureaucratic, rarely entertained. And yet it persists, quietly performing its function beneath the surface of institutional language. The difficulty, as ever, lies in classification. Students tend to interpret fatigue as either a failure of the environment or a failure of the self–either they have been asked to do too much, or they have failed to manage themselves appropriately. Both interpretations are plausible. Neither is particularly helpful. Fatigue is more accurately understood as a temporary reduction in the student's capacity to maintain competing narratives about their own importance. This is not a condition we should hastily correct. From this misreading emerge several familiar positions. The **physiological position** treats fatigue as a purely biological deficit–insufficient rest, excessive demand, a simple imbalance between input and recovery. Its strength lies in its clarity. Its weakness lies in its inability to account for the peculiar forms of insight that fatigue occasionally produces. The **psychological position** frames fatigue as burnout, a symptom of emotional overextension. It emphasises care, boundaries, and restoration. Its strength is its compassion. Its weakness is its tendency to stabilise the very structures that fatigue temporarily disrupts. The **institutional position**–often unspoken–treats fatigue as inefficiency. A tired student is a poorly performing unit within an otherwise functional system. Its strength is its operational simplicity. Its weakness is that it mistakes smooth functioning for meaningful activity. Each of these positions explains fatigue. None explains its utility. The matter, as ever, is structural. In a rested state, the student insists upon coherence: intention must precede action, and action must justify itself in language. Every mark must be defensible; every decision must be recoverable through explanation. They construct, with admirable diligence, a continuous narrative of authorship. Fatigue interrupts this continuity.

In a fatigued state, intention becomes diffuse, authorship uncertain, and meaning–most usefully–begins to detach itself from deliberate control. The student no longer maintains the illusion that every outcome was intended. Instead, things begin to happen.

Experientia accidit, non acquiritur. (Experience happens; it is not acquired.)

You will recognise the early symptoms. A small pedagogical observation, which I offer without enthusiasm for its replication: students experiencing moderate fatigue are approximately 52% more likely to describe minor aesthetic decisions as "profoundly intentional."

Non casu, sed consilio profundo. (Not by chance, but by deep design.)

This includes, but is not limited to, the accidental production of grey, the misplacement of sketchbooks, and the inability to locate one's own work within the studio. One student recently described an entirely unprimed canvas as "a refusal to impose surface hierarchy." It had, as far as I could determine, simply been forgotten. We must distinguish, however, between two forms of fatigue. **Productive fatigue** produces silence, occasional honesty, and brief moments of actual perception. The student looks, if only for a moment, without immediately converting what is seen into language. **Decorative fatigue**, by contrast, produces group messaging, performative vulnerability, and an alarming number of reflective statements beginning with "I think I'm learning that...". It is expressive, legible, and institutionally commendable. The University, naturally, has shown a consistent preference for the latter, as it is easier to document. Here, then, we arrive at the necessary inversion. Fatigue does not reduce meaning–it redistributes it. In a rested condition, students insist upon intention; in a fatigued condition, they begin to find intention everywhere. A failed composition becomes an "emergent structure"; a lack of ideas becomes "conceptual openness"; and a complete absence of output becomes a "resistance to commodified productivity." One almost wishes absence were more honest.

Nihil hic fortuitum. (Nothing here is accidental.)

And yet, something useful occurs within this excess of interpretation. Fatigue dismantles the student's editorial instincts. When sufficiently tired, they cease to distinguish between insight and phrasing. A sentence that feels correct becomes, by default, philosophically significant. This is how we arrive at the curious situation in which a student who has slept for four hours writes with the certainty of a minor prophet and the syntax of a press release. There is also a corresponding shift in their handling of materials. Fatigued students mix colours more freely, though not more accurately. They arrive, with some regularity, at a kind of universal grey–neither intentional nor entirely accidental–which they then defend as "tonal resolution." In truth, it is simply the point at which decision has collapsed into habit.

Ars eos portat, non ipsi artem. (Art carries them, not they art.)

A further observation: students are approximately 63% more likely to believe they are "on the verge of a breakthrough" when experiencing fatigue, provided they have also consumed excessive quantities of caffeine within the preceding three hours. This belief is remarkably stable, even in the absence of any observable progress. It should therefore be treated as a physiological condition rather than an intellectual one. We should not, however, mistake fatigue for weakness. Properly calibrated, it produces a kind of moral pliability that is exceptionally useful. The student no longer resists instruction so much as incorporates it into their exhaustion. At this stage, critique is no longer experienced as opposition; it becomes merely another texture in the general background of strain–like the hum of fluorescent lighting or the slow accumulation of unresolved canvases.

It is at this point that instruction becomes most effective, precisely because it is least noticeable. And yet, as with all useful conditions, fatigue must be carefully maintained. Excessive fatigue produces not humility, but a brittle and rather alarming certainty. The student begins to speak in absolutes, as though exhaustion had clarified rather than eroded their judgment. This is the point at which intervention becomes necessary–though not necessarily kindness. We must therefore sustain fatigue at a level that is neither restorative nor catastrophic. This is, admittedly, more difficult than it sounds, particularly given the University's fondness for scheduling enthusiasm at precisely the wrong biological intervals. I have long suspected that no student has ever improved during a nine o'clock critique, though many have convincingly pretended to, which is, I suppose, a transferable skill. What, then, is to be done? Very little, directly. Do not relieve fatigue prematurely. Do not dignify it excessively. Allow it to operate. For fatigue, when properly misunderstood, produces a condition of permeability. The student becomes less a creator of meaning than a surface through which meaning of uncertain origin briefly passes. If they recover too quickly, they will resume control. If they collapse entirely, they will withdraw. Our task, as ever, is to maintain them within that narrow and productive interval between the two. Thus, the final distinction: They believe fatigue is something happening to them. We understand it is something happening *through* them. They seek rest in order to regain control. We recognise that control is precisely what fatigue interrupts. And it is within that interruption that something–rare, unstable, and occasionally useful–may occur.

With appropriately moderated concern,

B. Judous

P.S.

I recall, with diminishing patience, a linear perspective class in which I presented the students with a perfectly ordinary problem: a model building, full scale; a ground plane; a fixed viewpoint, the corner A positioned two feet to the left of the spectator and one foot from the picture plane; the line AB vanishing to the right at an angle of forty degrees. The room, I regret to report, achieved a level of silence normally associated with religious contemplation. One student asked whether perspective was "still relevant to contemporary practice." Another suggested that vanishing points were "a form of imposed hierarchy."

P.P.S.

I have since concluded that perspective is not resisted because it is difficult, but because it implies that space behaves consistently–an idea which the modern student finds faintly oppressive.

Caute tractandum est. (It must be handled with caution.)

4

Dear Mr Jaded Muse,

There is, I have observed, a persistent and rather sentimental error among students entering this newly declared era of Art and creative thinking: they believe they own what they produce. The University, for its part, does little to discourage this belief. Ownership is, after all, administratively convenient. It allows for attribution, assessment, and–most importantly–accountability, all of which are considerably more difficult to maintain in the absence of clearly defined proprietors. One cannot grade an atmosphere, nor can one award marks to an event that refuses to identify its author. And so the language persists, quietly endorsed. I do not refer merely to legal ownership–which would be a minor administrative confusion, easily corrected with forms and signatures–but to a far more serious metaphysical claim: that the work of art is an extension of the self, rather than an event that happens to pass through it. It is, I concede, a comforting idea. And for that reason alone, it should be treated with caution.

Caute tractandum est. (It must be handled with caution.)

Students rarely arrive at this belief deliberately. It forms gradually, supported by a series of plausible assumptions: that intention precedes outcome, that expression originates internally, and that the finished work reflects, in some coherent way, the person who produced it. Each of these assumptions is, in isolation, defensible. Together, they produce a fiction that is remarkably difficult to dislodge. From this fiction emerge several interpretive positions. The **biographical position** proposes that the artwork is a manifestation of the self. It treats the work as evidence–something through which the inner life becomes visible. Its strength lies in its emotional accessibility. Its weakness is that it reduces the work to a symptom. The **formal position** rejects this entirely, insisting that the work should be understood independently of its maker. Structure, composition, material–these become the primary concerns. Its strength is its discipline. Its weakness is its occasional indifference to the conditions under which the work emerged. The **institutional position**–as ever–takes a more pragmatic approach. The work belongs to the student because it must. Without ownership, there can be no submission; without submission, no assessment; and without assessment, no progression. Its strength is its efficiency. Its weakness is that it confuses procedural necessity with ontological truth. Each position offers clarity. None offers stability. The difficulty, as you will have anticipated, is structural. Ownership implies continuity: a stable relationship between subject and object, intention and outcome, creator and work. Artistic practice, however, is defined precisely by its refusal to guarantee such continuity. The work does not proceed in a straight line from self to surface. It deviates, resists, accumulates, and occasionally exceeds the conditions of its making. The student, therefore, does not own the artwork. They occupy it. Intermittently, unevenly, and often with limited comprehension. Sometimes with clarity, sometimes with panic, occasionally with a kind of accidental grace. But always temporarily.

Non sunt domini, sed hospites. (They are not masters, but guests.)

You will have noticed the phrase appearing with increasing frequency in studio discourse: *my practice, my voice, my vision*. These are spoken with such solemnity that one might assume they had been issued by the University in embossed form, perhaps accompanied by a certificate and a modest fee. In reality, they function less as declarations than as defences–improvised protections against the more troubling possibility that nothing is actually possessed at all. This defensive function becomes particularly evident in relation to critique. A small pedagogical observation, offered in the spirit of professional curiosity: students who refer to a work as "mine" are approximately 58% more likely to resist critique, yet 73% more likely to exhibit that same work publicly before it is finished. The contradiction is not incidental; it is structural. Ownership, in their case, functions less as a claim of responsibility than as a justification for impatience. They defend what they have not yet understood. There is also the question of influence, which students handle with a charming absence of hierarchy. I have heard a student describe themselves as "owning" their influences, which is rather like claiming ownership of weather patterns because one has stood in the rain. Yet the language persists, because it allows them to convert inheritance into identity–a transformation that is rhetorically efficient, if conceptually fragile. And here, as before, material practice quietly contradicts their claims. A student layering paint upon a surface will speak of "building their image," as though the image were obedient to intention rather than resistant to it. In truth, the surface accumulates decisions that the student neither fully remembers nor entirely controls. The painting is not constructed; it is negotiated–often poorly.

Nihil hic fortuitum, sed multa non intellecta. (Nothing here is accidental, but much is not understood.)

At this point, one might be tempted to correct the misunderstanding directly–to inform the student that the work is not theirs, that authorship is unstable, that ownership is an illusion. This would be a mistake. Here, the inversion becomes necessary. The illusion of ownership, though false, is functionally useful. A student who believes their work is theirs also believes that success and failure are private events. This produces a level of emotional investment that would be difficult to generate under more accurate conditions. Without ownership, there is no urgency; without urgency, no output. The problem, therefore, is not ownership itself, but its stability. We must allow ownership to persist–but only in a weakened and inconsistent form. Let them say "my work," but ensure that what they mean by "my" shifts according to mood, weather, and proximity to deadlines. A stable pronoun is the first step towards artistic complacency.

"Meum" dicunt, sed sensum mutant. (They say "mine", but change its meaning.)

You will also observe that ownership, once established, becomes competitive. Students begin to compare possession as though it were a measurable resource. One student's confidence in their "voice" becomes another student's evidence of suppression. Thus, what begins as self-definition quickly degrades into comparative mythology. This competition produces its own visual symptoms. Students who feel insecure in their authorship often over-sign their work–literally or conceptually. They add marks, gestures, or excessive layers, not to resolve the image, but to insist upon presence. The result is not clarity, but saturation.

Quod additur non semper auget. (What is added does not always increase.)

A further pedagogical note: students exposed to sustained critique become approximately 41% more likely to reclassify failure as "conceptual positioning." This tendency peaks just before assessment deadlines, when reality becomes administratively inconvenient, and language must perform compensatory labour. And yet, beneath all of this, something more subtle persists. Students do not only believe they own the finished object; they believe they own the impulse that produced it. This is more dangerous. The impulse is, in reality, the least reliable participant in the entire process. It arrives late, departs early, and frequently refuses to identify itself. I once had a student insist that their lack of output was evidence of "protecting the purity of their vision." I suggested–perhaps unkindly–that their vision appeared to be on extended sabbatical, and had neglected to inform the department. The student responded by producing nothing further, which they later described as "consistency." The painting, as it happens, moved on without them. This, then, is the final distinction: They believe the work belongs to them. We understand they pass through it. They imagine ownership as a condition of control. We recognise it as a temporary alignment, already dissolving. And so, our task is not to remove ownership, but to destabilise its grammar. Let it remain as a habit of speech rather than a claim of fact. A student who is unsure what they own is far more attentive than one who believes everything is already accounted for.

Ars transit; discipulus manet. (Art passes through; the student remains.)

With measured detachment,

Mr B. Judous

5

Dear Mr Jaded Muse,

I find myself once again obliged to comment upon your students, who appear to be entering what I can only describe as a carefully unstructured phase of exhaustion. This is, I assure you, entirely satisfactory. Do not allow their complaints to mislead you into thinking that something has gone wrong; on the contrary, things are proceeding with an admirable lack of coherence, which, as you will come to understand, is precisely what the University tends to reward–provided, of course, it is properly documented. The institution has long maintained a quiet preference for processes that appear unstable but can be described convincingly after the fact. It is far easier to assess confusion that has been named than clarity that resists explanation. You report that they are "struggling to maintain momentum." This phrase, as you will discover, is less descriptive than aspirational. Momentum, in artistic education, is largely a retrospective fiction–constructed after the event by those who wish their earlier confusion to appear purposeful. It is rarely experienced in real time. A student never loses momentum. They merely discover, somewhat belatedly, that they never possessed it.

Motus fingitur post eventum. (Movement is invented after the event.)

This, then, is the central misreading: That artistic development proceeds through continuous forward motion. It is an attractive idea. It suggests direction, accumulation, and–most importantly–progress. Students speak of "building momentum," as though practice were governed by the same principles as rolling objects, requiring only sufficient force and minimal interruption. But such metaphors conceal more than they reveal. Let us consider the positions that support this belief. The **developmental position** assumes that artistic growth is incremental: each work improves upon the last, each decision contributes to a cumulative trajectory. Its strength lies in its optimism. Its weakness lies in its inability to account for regression, repetition, and the alarming frequency with which students appear to return to earlier states of confusion. The **motivational position**, favoured by those with an interest in productivity, treats momentum as a psychological resource. One must maintain energy, avoid interruption, and remain committed to forward movement. Its strength is its clarity. Its weakness is that it collapses when confronted with the realities of artistic hesitation. The **institutional position** quietly reinforces both, not because they are accurate, but because they are legible. A student who appears to be progressing is easier to assess than one who is circling, pausing, or–worse–standing still. Its strength is administrative efficiency. Its weakness is that it mistakes visibility for development. Each position depends upon the same assumption: That movement is continuous. It is not. The matter, as ever, is structural. Artistic practice does not proceed through momentum, but through interruption. Periods of activity are followed by hesitation, redirection, collapse, and occasional, inexplicable acceleration. What appears, in retrospect, as movement is in fact a series of discontinuities, later arranged into narrative for the sake of coherence. Momentum is not experienced. It is reconstructed. Under fatigue–as you have already observed–this reconstruction becomes more difficult to maintain. Fatigue does not interrupt momentum; it reveals its absence. In a fatigued state, intention loosens, control weakens, and the student becomes–if only briefly–less concerned with maintaining the appearance of continuity. The work no longer pretends to be part of a sequence. It simply occurs. This is not comfortable, but it is useful. A curious pedagogical observation for you: students under moderate fatigue exhibit approximately a 63% increase in what they describe as "emotional honesty." This is to say, they become dramatically more willing to produce work that is unfinished, poorly considered, and subsequently defended as "raw." We encourage this, within limits. Rawness, as you will learn, is simply incompetence with better lighting.

Cruditas non est veritas. (Rawness is not truth.)

You will notice that such work often involves a sudden abandonment of structure–looser marks, thinner paint, larger gestures–accompanied by language that suggests intentional release rather than technical collapse. One student recently described an unprimed, sagging canvas as "refusing containment." It was, in fact, refusing preparation. At this point, one might be tempted to restore order–to encourage clarity, to reintroduce structure, to guide the student back toward a more recognisable trajectory. This would be premature. Here, the inversion becomes necessary. Recovery is not always desirable. Recovery leads to clarity. Clarity leads to judgment. Judgement leads, inevitably, to students asking whether they should perhaps "revise their practice"–which is the first stage in a long and tedious process we refer to internally as thinking for oneself.

Cogitare incipiunt—periculum est. (They begin to think—this is dangerous.)

You mention that some students have begun to oscillate between hope and despair. This is, as you correctly suspect, ideal. Hope is merely despair with better posture; despair is hope without its administrative approval. The important thing is not which they experience, but that they remain sufficiently preoccupied by the alternation to avoid noticing that neither state produces work on its own. Between the two lies a narrow but productive corridor–one in which the student continues to act without fully understanding why. It is here that most of their work, such as it is, will emerge. Allow me a further observation. When students are told that improvement is possible, they tend to assume it is imminent. This is unfortunate, but entirely predictable. We then spend the following months managing their disappointment as though it were a technical fault in the curriculum, rather than a misunderstanding of time itself.

Tempus non accelerat ad voluntatem. (Time does not hasten according to desire.)

The average student believes "next week" to be a meaningful artistic horizon. In reality, it functions more like a psychological storage cupboard–useful for postponing confrontation with anything unresolved, while giving the reassuring impression of organisation. You are also to be commended–though only cautiously–for your handling of their recent “creative crises.” These episodes, in which students briefly believe they have lost their artistic identity, should not be resolved too quickly. Identity loss is one of the few experiences that reliably produces both writing and attendance, and occasionally even looking. However, I must caution you against offering reassurance that is too coherent. Reassurance, when clearly formulated, becomes instruction. Instruction, when too precise, becomes resistance training. And resistance training produces students who begin to suspect they are stronger than the system upon which they remain entirely dependent. We must avoid producing resilient students. Resilience, in excess, leads to independence, and independence is notoriously difficult to assess.

Independentia vix aestimatur. (Independence is scarcely assessable.)

There is also the matter of their increasing attachment to feedback. You may already have observed this: they no longer treat critique as information, but as weather–something to be endured, discussed at length, and blamed when inconvenient. I once had a student ask me whether their painting was “a good Tuesday piece or a bad Thursday piece.” I have, I confess, not entirely recovered from the question. There is, however, a visual counterpart to this behaviour. Students awaiting feedback often cease making decisions altogether. The work hovers in a state of suspended intention–neither resolved nor abandoned–like a painting paused mid-sentence. They refer to this as "holding space." It is, more accurately, a form of controlled hesitation.

Suspensio non est resolutio. (Suspension is not resolution.)

And so, we arrive at the pedagogical instruction, though it must never appear as such: Do not restore their sense of direction. Do not confirm the existence of momentum. Allow them instead to experience movement as intermittent, uncertain, and only retrospectively meaningful. For it is in this condition that they remain most productive–not because they are progressing, but because they cannot yet prove that they are not. Thus, the final distinction: They believe they are moving forward. We understand they are being moved through phases. They seek momentum as evidence of progress. We recognise it as a narrative constructed to survive confusion. And so, we teach them–not to arrive–but to remain convincingly in transit.

In transitu manent, non perveniunt. (They remain in transit; they do not arrive.)

Yours in managed exhaustion,

B. Tudorg

6

Dear Mr Jaded Muse,

I am informed–though never reliably, and certainly never without embellishment–that your students have begun to exhibit an unfortunate sensitivity to critique. This is not, as you may assume, a developmental setback. It is, rather, an early and promising indication that they are beginning to recognise criticism as something that applies to them personally, rather than as an abstract atmospheric condition affecting only other, more talented cohorts. The University, as you will discover, prefers critique to remain atmospheric for as long as possible. It circulates best when it is not yet recognised as directed. Once it becomes personal, however, it begins to acquire weight. Students notice it. They react to it. Occasionally, they even remember it. We must be careful here. Sensitivity is not in itself undesirable; it is merely unfinished perception. The danger lies not in feeling too much, but in allowing feeling to settle prematurely into comprehension.

Sensus sine intellectu utilis est. (Feeling without understanding is useful.)

This, then, is the central misreading: That critique is a statement about the self, rather than a condition through which the work is temporarily exposed. Students tend to interpret critique in two primary ways, both of which are equally inaccurate and equally productive. From this misreading emerge several positions. The **evaluative**

position treats critique as a verdict. The work is judged, and by extension, so is the student. Its strength lies in its clarity. Its weakness is that it collapses the distinction between object and subject, making all feedback feel terminal. The **relational position** interprets critique as an act of care or betrayal. Feedback is no longer information, but a gesture–either supportive or hostile. Its strength is its emotional sensitivity. Its weakness is that it renders accuracy secondary to tone. The **performative position**, increasingly common, treats critique as an opportunity for visible engagement. The student responds, reframes, resists–demonstrating participation rather than processing information. Its strength is its fluency. Its weakness is that it often leaves the work unchanged. Each position captures something of the experience of critique. None captures its function. The matter, as ever, is structural. Critique is not a message. It is an interruption. It interrupts the student's internal narrative about what the work is, what it was intended to be, and–most importantly–what it has already been decided to mean. This interruption is rarely welcome. It is, however, necessary. And so, students respond as one might expect. A neutral observation becomes an existential indictment; a suggestion becomes an assault; and silence–silence is invariably interpreted as contempt, which is particularly convenient for those of us who occasionally forget to reply. There is, as you will have noticed, a visual analogue to this behaviour. Students who feel "attacked" by critique often respond by overworking their surfaces–adding marks, layers, gestures–not to resolve the work, but to defend it. The painting thickens; the thinking does not.

Quod additur non semper auget. (What is added does not always increase.)

A useful pedagogical observation: students retain approximately 71% more of negative feedback when it is delivered indirectly–preferably after they have already decided they were doing well. This is why I tend to begin most critiques with the phrase, “there is something rather promising here,” which functions less as encouragement than as a preparatory trapdoor. Expectation, once elevated, falls with greater force. It is worth noting that critique is most effective not when it is understood, but when it is misremembered. A student who fully comprehends feedback may incorporate it. A student who partially misunderstands it will reorganise their entire approach around it, often with far more dramatic results. And yet, we must proceed cautiously with praise. Praise, as you will learn, is not nourishment–it is fermentation. Left unchecked, it produces a volatile confidence which students are then compelled to interpret as talent. Once this interpretation has taken hold, all subsequent instruction is experienced as interference.

Laus corrumpit, nisi temperetur. (Praise corrupts, unless it is tempered.)

I once had a student who, after receiving a single compliment on their use of colour, attempted to reframe their entire practice as “chromatic epistemology.” They subsequently produced nothing for eight months, though they did speak with increasing authority during group critiques. The University, I regret to report, recorded this as “professional development.” You will find that colour is particularly susceptible to this inflation. A student who accidentally arrives at a compelling relationship between two tones will immediately assume authorship of the phenomenon, and then spend the remainder of the term attempting to reproduce what was never entirely theirs to begin with. The result is not mastery, but repetition under pressure.

Repetitio non est intelligentia. (Repetition is not understanding.)

At this point, one might be tempted to clarify–to explain the nature of critique, to reassure the student that feedback is not personal, to restore a sense of stability. This would be unwise. Here, the inversion becomes necessary. Critique must remain partially misunderstood in order to remain effective. A student who fully understands critique becomes selective. They accept what aligns with their existing framework and reject what does not. A student who does not understand critique remains open–if only because they cannot yet determine what to ignore. Misunderstanding, in this context, is not a failure. It is a condition of permeability. You will also observe that students begin, at this stage, to test authority in small, decorative ways. They do this by asking questions that appear intellectual but are, in fact, procedural negotiations: "Do we have to follow this brief?" "Is this assessment really necessary?" "What if I ignore the constraints entirely and explain why afterwards?" These are not questions. They are invitations to dissolve structure. You must not accept them. To answer directly would be to acknowledge that the structure exists for their benefit–a misconception we have worked diligently to avoid. Instead, respond with a degree of ambiguity that suggests both inevitability and personal responsibility, preferably in equal measure. Authority, properly maintained, should resemble weather: sometimes visible, occasionally oppressive, but never negotiable.

Auctoritas non explicatur—sentitur. (Authority is not explained—it is felt.)

A further observation, offered more as warning than advice: students who begin to "challenge the brief" rarely stop at the brief. They proceed, with admirable enthusiasm, to challenge time, coherence, and eventually their own ability to complete anything resembling a finished thought. At that point, we describe them–somewhat generously–as "conceptually engaged." There is also a corresponding visual pattern. Students who claim to be "questioning the framework" often produce work that avoids decision entirely. Edges remain unresolved, compositions drift, and materials are left in a state of suspended intention. They refer to this as openness. It is, more accurately, hesitation with theoretical support.

Suspensio non est libertas. (Suspension is not freedom.)

And yet, we must allow a certain degree of resistance to persist. A student who never questions critique becomes passive. A student who rejects it entirely becomes unreachable. The useful position lies somewhere in between: partial disagreement, inconsistently applied. The average student believes that disagreement with feedback is a form of artistic maturity. In reality, it is usually nothing more than a delay in wearing intellectual clothing. Nevertheless, a small amount of disagreement should be permitted to flourish. It provides them with the comforting illusion that they are participating in their own education, rather than being slowly processed by it. Participation, as you will learn, need not be genuine to be effective.

Illusio participationis sufficit. (The illusion of participation is sufficient.)

Thus, the final distinction: They believe critique is something done *to* them. We understand it is something that happens *between* them and the work. They seek clarity in feedback. We preserve its instability. And so, our task is not to silence them, but to ensure that what they say does not arrive in the correct order.

Ordo perturbandus est. (The order must be disturbed.)

Yours in calibrated authority,

B. Judous

7

Dear Mr Jaded Muse,

It has come to my attention via a chain of increasingly unreliable intermediaries, including a visiting critic, a misfiled email, and a student who believes punctuation is a form of oppression, that collaboration is once again being encouraged in your studios. I must ask, with the weary affection of someone who has watched this cycle repeat itself with the regularity of term dates, whether we have learned nothing. The University has always maintained a cautious enthusiasm for collaboration. It photographs well, distributes responsibility efficiently, and produces the appearance of collective engagement without requiring the inconvenience of individual certainty. For these reasons alone, it is unlikely to disappear. Students, naturally, receive it with immediate optimism. This optimism, as you will have anticipated, is misplaced. Collaboration, in theory, is presented as a noble alignment of creative forces. In practice, it is what occurs when individual uncertainty discovers it is not alone. The result is not synthesis, but mutual reassurance disguised as production. One might compare it to several mediocre singers attempting harmony without first agreeing on the song; the outcome is not music, but a polite acoustic misunderstanding. This, then, is the central misreading: That collaboration produces depth through agreement. It is an appealing belief. It suggests that multiple perspectives will converge, that differences will enrich the outcome, and that shared effort will produce something greater than the sum of its parts. It rarely does. From this belief emerge several positions. The **collective position** argues that collaboration expands creative possibilities. By combining perspectives, students access ideas unavailable to them individually. Its strength lies in its generosity. Its weakness is that it assumes difference will be preserved rather than negotiated into disappearance. The **social position** treats collaboration as a necessary condition of contemporary practice. Artists must work together, respond to one another, and operate within networks. Its strength is its realism. Its weakness is that it often confuses participation with contribution. The **institutional position**, predictably, values collaboration for its legibility. Group work produces documentation, dialogue, and measurable interaction–all of which can be assessed. Its strength is its efficiency. Its weakness is that it rewards process regardless of outcome. Each position contains a degree of truth. None accounts for what actually happens. The matter, as ever, is structural. Collaboration does not amplify conviction–it redistributes uncertainty. When multiple students work together, decisions are no longer made through clarity but through negotiation. Each participant adjusts, concedes, and reframes until the work reflects not the strongest idea, but the least resisted one.

Consensus sine intellectu. (Agreement without understanding.)

A useful pedagogical fact: in groups of three or more, the probability of a student abandoning a coherent idea in favour of a collectively "interesting direction" increases by approximately 58%. The remaining percentage is usually spent deciding what "interesting" might mean, though it rarely survives definition. You will also notice that collaboration allows students to outsource both conviction and responsibility simultaneously. It is, in this sense, the perfect educational technology. No one is entirely accountable for the failure, and everyone is partially responsible for the confusion. It is democracy in its most aesthetically unproductive form. I once observed a group of students produce what they described–without visible hesitation–as a "shared visual language."

Communis lingua imaginum—sed male intellecta. (A shared language of images—badly understood.)

What they had, in fact, produced was a surface in which every decision had been negotiated to the point of neutrality: a colour palette that appeared to apologise for itself, a composition that refused to privilege any element, and a scale that suggested ambition while committing to none. When I asked who had made which decision, they looked at one another with the expression of people attempting to recall a dream they had all agreed to forget. There is, incidentally, a material signature to collaborative work. Edges soften, contrasts diminish, and colour relationships drift toward compromise. Strong colours rarely survive committee; they are either diluted or displaced. One rarely sees a decisive red in a group project –it is softened into something more agreeable or justified retrospectively as "too dominant."

Rubrum recusatur ubi omnes audiuntur. (Red is refused where all must be heard.)

At this point, one might be tempted to discourage collaboration entirely. This would be both impractical and, more importantly, suspicious. Here, the inversion becomes necessary. Collaboration must not be removed. It must be maintained in a state of controlled instability. Students should feel that they are building something together while quietly suspecting that none of them would have chosen it alone. This suspicion is essential. Without it, they might begin to trust the outcome. Trust, in this context, is far more dangerous than confusion. You will also observe that students begin to mistake agreement for depth. If two concur, they assume understanding. If five concur, they assume art has been made. In reality, they have simply reduced friction to the point where nothing sufficiently resistant can occur.

Frictione carente, nihil fit. (Without friction, nothing happens.)

A minor observation from recent critiques: the most collaborative groups tend to produce the least revisable work. Not because it is finished, but because no one is willing to admit where it begins or ends. It exists instead in a permanent state of collective authorship–like a rumour that has lost its origin but retained its confidence. You will also notice the emergence of moral language around these processes. Students begin to speak of "respecting each voice," which is admirable in principle but disastrous in execution. Too many voices, properly respected, produce a kind of aesthetic paralysis in which every decision is deferred, and every deferral is justified. Respect, in excess, becomes postponement.

Respectus nimis dilatio fit. (Excessive respect becomes delay.)

There is also a quieter danger, which I urge you to observe closely: the emergence of the group-identity artist. This species produces less and affiliates more. Their portfolio becomes a sequence of memberships, residencies, and collective statements–each more linguistically refined than the last, and none requiring the inconvenience of solitary failure.

Societas pro opere ponitur. (Association replaces work.)

If I sound unsympathetic, it is only because I have spent too many years watching promising solitude dissolve into agreeable noise. And yet–here we must allow for a complication. Occasionally, very occasionally, something resembling genuine insight does emerge from collaboration. It tends to occur not because of the group, but in spite of it–usually at the precise moment when one student ceases to agree and another forgets to apologise. In that brief interval, negotiation collapses, and something like authorship reappears.

Auctor nascitur in discordia. (Authorship is born in disagreement.)

We should, perhaps, allow for these accidents–though never rely upon them. Thus, the final distinction: They believe collaboration produces shared vision. We understand it produces negotiated uncertainty. They seek agreement as a form of validation. We preserve disagreement as a condition of clarity.

And so, our task is not to prevent collaboration, but to ensure that it never becomes comfortable enough to be mistaken for understanding.

Yours in structured scepticism,

B. Judous

8

Dear Mr Jaded Muse,

I write to you today in a state of what I can only describe as professionally moderated despair, having once again been presented with your recent assessment of student "talent"–a term which I have long suspected is less an observation than an administrative convenience for avoiding detailed thought. The University, as you will have noticed, requires such terms. Without them, we would be forced into the far more demanding task of describing what students actually do, rather than what we believe they are. "Talent" functions, therefore, not as a conclusion, but as a placeholder–a way of suspending judgement while appearing to exercise it. You appear, in your report, to have identified a small number of "gifted" individuals, a larger number of "developing" ones, and a residual category best described as "unclear but present." This taxonomy is charmingly optimistic in much the same way that early cartography was optimistic about the existence of sea monsters.

An monstra sint? Discipuli negant, donec fiant. (Do monsters exist? Students deny it—until they become them.)

This, then, is the central misreading: That talent is a stable attribute which can be identified early, classified reliably, and used to predict future development. It is an attractive belief. It allows us to sort, to rank, and–most importantly–to reassure ourselves that the system is capable of recognising quality when it appears. It rarely is. From this belief emerge several positions. The **natural ability position** assumes that talent is innate–a quality possessed by some and absent in others. Its strength lies in its simplicity. Its weakness lies in its inconsistency, particularly when those identified as talented fail to produce anything of interest. The **developmental position** reframes talent as potential–something that may not yet be visible but can be cultivated through effort. Its strength is its generosity. Its weakness is that it often extends indefinitely, producing students who are permanently "developing" without ever arriving. The **institutional position**, as you might expect, treats talent as a classification tool. It allows for differentiation, recognition, and the efficient distribution of attention. Its strength is its utility. Its weakness is that it quietly confuses recognition with existence. Each position offers a way of speaking about talent. None explains how it behaves. The difficulty, as you are beginning to suspect, is that talent is not distributed in any legible manner. It arrives irregularly, behaves inconsistently, and–most inconveniently of all–refuses to correspond to effort. This makes it deeply unpopular in academic settings, where we prefer qualities that can be timetabled, measured, and–if necessary–reassuringly misunderstood. A useful pedagogical observation for your consideration: students who are told they possess "natural talent" exhibit approximately a 37% decrease in sustained practice within three weeks, and a corresponding 52% increase in describing themselves as "in a process." The phrase, as you will come to recognise, is where work goes to become socially unassailable and practically absent.

Processus dicitur ubi opus deficit. ("Process" is invoked where work is lacking.)

You will notice that such students begin to substitute articulation for production. They speak with increasing confidence about what the work is "doing," even as the work itself becomes progressively less present. It is at this stage that language ceases to describe practice and begins to replace it. There is, incidentally, a visual correlate to this condition. Students who believe themselves to be "talented" tend to increase scale prematurely–larger canvases, broader gestures, more ambitious formats–without a corresponding increase in structural understanding. The result is not expansion, but amplification of uncertainty.

Amplificatio sine structura nihil est. (Expansion without structure is nothing.)

And yet, here we must pause. It would be tempting–dangerously so–to abandon the concept of talent altogether. To declare it meaningless, to remove it from our vocabulary, and to proceed with a more equitable, if less efficient, system of evaluation. This would be an error. Here, the inversion becomes necessary. Talent, though unstable, is functionally useful. The University's relationship with talent has always been one of quiet mismanagement. We discover it, praise it, isolate it, overexpose it to critique, and then express surprise when it either collapses or migrates elsewhere. I once observed a particularly promising student leave the programme entirely after being described as "exceptional but not yet coherent," which is, I suspect, also how one might describe a slightly alarming soup. And yet, despite this, the concept persists. Why? Because the illusion of talent produces behaviour. A student who believes they have been recognised will continue to produce in the hope of being recognised again. A student who believes they lack talent will either withdraw or compensate–both of which generate observable outcomes. Talent, in this sense, is less a quality than a mechanism.

Consensus facit talentum. (Agreement makes talent.)

There is also the matter of misdiagnosis, which occurs with distressing frequency in early assessments. Students who are merely articulate are mistaken for insightful; students who are visually loud are mistaken for visually competent; and students who speak in complete sentences during critique are often promoted–informally, but decisively–to "future practitioners."

Loquuntur ergo creduntur. (They speak, therefore they are believed.)

One must therefore ask whether we are identifying talent or merely identifying students who are particularly fluent in the language of being identified. This fluency, as you will have observed, is highly adaptive. It allows students to survive critique without ever fully encountering it. They learn, with admirable speed, that if one speaks about one's work with sufficient abstraction, the work itself becomes optional. "Exploration." "Interrogation." "Practice-led inquiry." All admirable phrases. All equally capable of concealing absence.

Verba tegunt, non mutant. (Words conceal; they do not change.)

And yet, we must proceed carefully. If we strip away all notions of talent, we are left with something far more troubling: responsibility. Responsibility requires the student to account for what is produced, rather than what might be possible. It introduces a clarity that is, in many cases, unwelcome. Students confronted with responsibility tend to produce less rhetoric and more hesitation–a condition which the University has historically struggled to quantify. Hesitation, unlike talent, resists classification. A final observation, offered as both curiosity and caution: Students who believe themselves to be "not talented but hardworking" tend, in the long term, to outperform both categories. They do so, however, with significantly less happiness and a worrying tendency to describe themselves as "late bloomers"–as though art were horticulture with emotional invoices attached.

Lente crescunt, sed crescunt. (They grow slowly, but they grow.)

And so, we arrive at the necessary distinction: They believe talent is something one possesses. We understand it is something temporarily agreed upon. They seek recognition as confirmation of ability. We recognise recognition as a condition that produces behaviour. And so, we must continue–carefully, inconsistently–to name talent, withdraw it, redistribute it, and occasionally pretend it was never there. For we are not, after all, identifying artists. We are maintaining a belief system about them.

With calibrated scepticism,

B. Judous

9

Dear Mr Jaded Muse,

I have received your latest reflections on student "failure", a term you employ with such administrative neutrality that one might be forgiven for imagining it refers to a misplaced folder rather than a young person's entire sense of artistic existence. The University, as you will have noticed, prefers failure when it is linguistically subdued. It can then be filed, referenced, and–if necessary–reframed as "development." Once named too precisely, however, it becomes inconvenient. Students begin to recognise it, tutors begin to account for it, and the entire system risks becoming momentarily honest. You express concern that several students are "struggling to produce viable outcomes." I must gently remind you that viability is not, and has never been, the primary currency of artistic education. Indeed, if viability were our aim, we would long ago have replaced the studio with a modestly efficient accounting suite and instructed students in the delicate art of spreadsheets rendered in soft greys. This, then, is the central misreading: That failure is a deviation from learning, rather than its primary condition. It is an understandable belief. Failure presents itself with such clarity–an unsuccessful work, an unresolved outcome, an unconvincing explanation–that one assumes it requires correction. Yet in the context of artistic formation, correction is rarely the most useful response. Failure, properly understood, is not an interruption of their learning; it is the learning itself, merely arriving without the courtesy of explanation.

Cadere docet sine ratione. (Failure teaches without explanation.)

From this misreading emerge several positions. The **corrective position** treats failure as a problem to be solved. One identifies the error, adjusts the method, and produces a better outcome. Its strength lies in its practicality. Its weakness is that it assumes the goal is improvement rather than transformation. The **reflective position** reframes failure as an opportunity for insight. Students are encouraged to analyse what went wrong and extract meaning from it. Its strength is its thoughtfulness. Its weakness is that it stabilises failure too quickly, converting it into narrative before it has done its work. The **institutional position**, predictably, treats failure as a metric. It is recorded, contextualised, and–where possible mitigated. Its strength is its orderliness. Its weakness is that it reduces an unstable condition to a manageable category. Each position attempts to contain failure. None allows it to operate. The matter, as ever, is structural. Failure functions not by being understood, but by remaining partially illegible. A student who fully understands their failure can begin to correct it. A student who cannot yet explain it remains within its influence, adjusting, reacting, and–most importantly–continuing to produce. This is why failure must resist definition.

Definitio est periculum. (Definition is danger.)

A useful pedagogical observation: students who experience repeated minor failures without resolution show approximately a 44% increase in conceptual ambition and a 61% decrease in willingness to reattempt the same task.

This is, of course, ideal. We want ambition unburdened by repetition. Repetition leads to craft. Craft leads to competence. Competence, as you know, is indistinguishable from closure–and closure is death to the properly unstable artist. And yet, we must be cautious. There is a secondary misreading, one that emerges once failure becomes familiar. Students begin to identify with it. You will recognise this immediately. Students begin to describe themselves as "struggling artists," not as a temporary condition but as a stable identity–something inherited, curated, and, in certain cases, quietly admired. This is dangerous. Not because it is untrue, but because it is stabilising. A student who has fully accepted their failure becomes oddly calm. They stop asking for reassurance, stop seeking critique, and begin producing work that is–worryingly–consistent. Consistency, I should remind you, is merely failure without surprise.

Constans est defectus sine casu. (Consistency is failure without accident.)

Allow me to illustrate. I once observed a student produce what was, by any reasonable metric, a catastrophic outcome: a painting that appeared to have been negotiated between three incompatible moods and a malfunctioning light source. The surface was neither resolved nor unresolved, but suspended in a state of accidental hostility. The student, however, described it as "a successful deconstruction of painterly authority." It was at that moment I realised we had achieved something important: Failure had been successfully reclassified as intention. This is, I assure you, the correct direction of travel. And yet–here, as always, the inversion must be applied carefully. We must allow failure to be reinterpreted, but not resolved. A small administrative curiosity: students who are reassured too frequently about the "value of failure" begin to treat it as a form of achievement. They will say things such as, "I failed in a really interesting way this time," which is roughly equivalent to congratulating oneself on having fallen down with conceptual coherence. We must resist the transformation of failure into style. Style, once established, is simply repetition with better lighting. There is also the matter of recovery. Recovery from failure is, pedagogically speaking, far more problematic than failure itself. It introduces narrative. And narrative encourages students to believe they are progressing through something, rather than being continuously reshaped by it. We do not want progress. Progress implies direction. Direction implies arrival. Arrival implies assessment. And assessment, as you have already learned, is where illusions go to be marked down.

Progressus ducit ad finem. (Progress leads to an end.)

And so, our task is not to eliminate failure, nor to celebrate it excessively, but to maintain it in a state of productive ambiguity. Failure must remain slightly embarrassing, occasionally enlightening, and never fully explainable. For when failure becomes articulate, it ceases to be useful.

Quod explicatur, dissolvitur. (What is explained, dissolves.)

Thus, the final distinction: They believe failure is something to be overcome. We understand it is something to be sustained. They seek to explain it in order to survive it. We preserve its opacity in order to extend it. And it is within this extended, unresolved condition that the only work worth considering tends, eventually, to emerge.

Yours in productive instability,

10

Dear Mr Jaded Muse,

I have noted, with a mixture of professional interest and personal fatigue, your concerns regarding students' "time management." This phrase alone would be sufficient to warrant an entire symposium, preferably held somewhere mildly uncomfortable, so that at least the environment would not contradict the subject matter. The University, as you will have observed, is deeply invested in the fiction that time can be organised. Timetables are produced, schedules circulated, and deadlines announced with an air of quiet authority, as though time itself had agreed to participate. It has not. You write as though time were a resource distributed fairly, or worse, one that might be sensibly organised. I can only assume you have never observed a student in possession of it. This, then, is the central misreading: That time is something students have, rather than something they intermittently experience. A student does not manage time; they negotiate with it, misplace it, apologise to it, and ultimately accuse it of betrayal. Time, in return, proceeds entirely unaffected.

Tempus non respondet. (Time does not respond.)

From this misreading emerge several positions. The **organisational position** assumes that time can be structured. With sufficient planning, prioritisation, and discipline, students will allocate hours effectively and produce consistent outcomes. Its strength lies in its clarity.

Its weakness is that it collapses upon contact with actual behaviour. The **moral position** interprets time management as a question of character. To use time well is to be responsible; to waste it is to be deficient. Its strength lies in its motivational force. Its weakness is that it produces guilt more reliably than work. The **institutional position**, as ever, treats time as measurable. Hours are logged, attendance recorded, and deadlines enforced. Its strength is its visibility. Its weakness is that it confuses compliance with engagement. Each position attempts to stabilise time. None succeeds. The matter, as ever, is structural. Students do not possess time. They pass through it, intermittently aware, frequently disoriented, and occasionally convinced that they have briefly understood its arrangement.

Illusio possessionis temporis. (The illusion of owning time.)

A useful pedagogical observation: when students are asked to "use their time effectively," approximately 68% interpret this as a moral instruction rather than a practical one. The result is what we term *productive guilt cycles*–states in which no work is produced, but exhaustion is nonetheless achieved. This is, as you might imagine, a form of institutional efficiency. You will have observed that nothing destabilises a student more effectively than the discovery that their time is not aligned with their intentions. They begin each term believing they have been granted a continuous, usable stretch of existence. By week three, they are attempting to subdivide it into "studio time," "thinking time," "recovery time," and–most poignantly–"time I will definitely catch up later." Here we encounter a secondary misreading: That "later" is a reliable extension of the present. It is not. "Later" is not a period of time; it is an emotional storage facility. It exists to house intentions that would otherwise be forced to confront the present.

Posteritas est refugium voluntatis. ("Later" is the refuge of intention.)

There is also the phenomenon of borrowed urgency. This occurs when students, having neglected a task for several weeks, suddenly believe the remaining hours have increased in intensity to compensate. They will say things such as, "I work better under pressure," which is simply panic translated into optimism for administrative consumption.

Stressus vocatur efficacia. (Stress is called efficiency.)

A further observation from long experience: students consistently overestimate the stability of "later," while underestimating the volatility of "now." The present, when encountered directly, has a tendency to collapse under scrutiny. It resists organisation, refuses extension, and–most inconveniently–demands decision. It is for this reason that students avoid it. At this point, one might be tempted to correct the misunderstanding–to teach students how to structure their time, to plan effectively, to align intention with action. This would be a mistake. Here, the inversion becomes necessary. We must preserve the illusion of temporal control while quietly ensuring its failure. It is essential that students continue to believe they possess time, even as they repeatedly encounter evidence to the contrary. The resulting instability produces a condition in which they remain active–not because they are organised, but because they are perpetually attempting to become so.

You also mention, almost in passing, that some students appear "disorganised but intensely engaged." I would advise you not to confuse engagement with structure. A student can be deeply engaged in the same way a room can be deeply on fire: illuminating, chaotic, and temporarily impressive, but not necessarily suitable for habitation. There is, in fact, a distinct visual signature to this condition. Works produced under temporal panic tend to accumulate gestures rather than decisions–brushstrokes multiply, surfaces overheat, and composition becomes a record of urgency rather than thought. The result is not clarity, but velocity mistaken for meaning.

Motus non est forma. (Movement is not form.)

We should also address their growing tendency to treat deadlines as philosophical propositions rather than administrative facts. I recently encountered a student who described a missed submission as "a temporal intervention in my practice." I have ensured, where possible, that they will be reminded of reality at irregular intervals. A minor diagnostic observation: students who refer to deadlines as "fluid" are approximately 49% more likely to submit work that reflects this condition–unfinished, unstable, and accompanied by a statement explaining why completion would have been conceptually inappropriate. Completion, as you will recall, is rarely fashionable. And yet–here we must allow for a complication. Students do occasionally produce their most compelling work when time is visibly collapsing around them. This should not be mistaken for a virtue. It is merely the aesthetic by-product of panic achieving temporary coherence.

Coactio non est creatio. (Coercion is not creation.)

We must resist the temptation to institutionalise this condition. Panic, once formalised, becomes expectation. Expectation, once stabilised, becomes method. And method, as you know, is where unpredictability goes to disappear. And so, we arrive at the necessary instruction, though it must remain indirect: Do not teach students how to use time well. Instead, ensure that they remain uncertain as to whether they have used it at all. A student who believes they are always slightly late will continue moving. A student who believes they are on time will begin to interpret stillness as achievement. We cannot allow that.

Stabilitas est periculum. (Stability is danger.)

Thus, the final distinction: They believe time is something to be managed. We understand it is something that resists management. They seek alignment between intention and duration. We preserve the misalignment that produces action. And it is within this misalignment–persistent, irritating, and never quite resolved–that all useful work continues to occur.

Yours in temporal administration,

B. Judong

11

Dear Mr Jaded Muse,

I have read, with a kind of exhausted fascination, your remarks concerning the students' "struggle for originality." It is, I assure you, one of the more predictable symptoms of the current academic climate, appearing with the regularity of seasonal allergies and producing roughly the same degree of discomfort in all involved–though, curiously, never enough to prevent its recurrence. The University, as you will have observed, continues to invoke originality with a ceremonial seriousness that far exceeds its operational clarity. It appears in briefs, assessment criteria, and visiting lectures with equal authority, despite the persistent absence of any stable definition. Students are told to pursue it, tutors are asked to recognise it, and committees are required to measure it–all without ever agreeing on what it might be. This, then, is the central misreading: That originality is a property that can be intentionally produced. You write as though originality were a substance they might eventually acquire through sufficient effort, like varnish, competence, or a particularly well-behaved pigment. This is a charming misconception, and one I would discourage you from correcting too abruptly. Students must be permitted to believe that originality is both attainable and recognisable. Without this belief, they might begin to suspect the truth: that originality is largely a retrospective judgement made by people who were not present at the moment of its production.

Originalitas post eventum cognoscitur. (Originality is recognised after the event.)

From this misreading emerge several positions. The **expressive position** assumes that originality arises from authenticity. If one is sufficiently true to oneself, the work will naturally differ from that of others. Its strength lies in its sincerity. Its weakness is that the "self" it relies upon is neither stable nor particularly original. The **innovative position** treats originality as novelty. One must produce something new–visually, conceptually, or materially–in order to distinguish oneself. Its strength is its clarity. Its weakness is that novelty is quickly exhausted and even more quickly imitated. The **institutional position**, predictably, treats originality as a criterion. It must be identified, described, and rewarded, despite its resistance to definition. Its strength is its necessity. Its weakness is that it produces agreement without understanding. Each position offers a method for pursuing originality. None explains how it appears. The matter, as ever, is structural. Originality is not produced through intention, but recognised through difference–and difference is rarely visible at the moment of its making. The student, therefore, cannot reliably determine whether what they are doing is original. They can only attempt to avoid resemblance. This leads, quite predictably, to imitation of a particular kind. A useful pedagogical fact: students who are explicitly instructed to "be original" demonstrate approximately a 72% increase in stylistic imitation within two weeks. The instruction does not fail; it succeeds too efficiently, redirecting attention from making toward avoidance of resemblance, which is itself a more sophisticated form of resemblance. They do not imitate others. They imitate the gesture of not imitating. You will also have noticed their growing horror of repetition. They speak of it as though it were a moral failing rather than the fundamental condition of all artistic practice. Nothing reveals a student's insecurity more clearly than their belief that repetition indicates stagnation rather than survival.

Repetitio non est defectus sed fundamentum. (Repetition is not failure but foundation.)

In truth, repetition is where most work quietly becomes itself. It produces familiarity, exposes structure, and allows decisions to accumulate into something resembling intention. Without repetition, there is no continuity; without continuity, no development. And yet–we must proceed carefully. If students are allowed to become comfortable with repetition, they risk developing something dangerously close to craft. And craft, as you know, is merely originality that has stopped apologising. Here, then, we arrive at the necessary inversion. Repetition must be both permitted and resisted. Encourage it sufficiently to produce coherence, but interrupt it before it stabilises into method. A student who repeats without awareness becomes mechanical; a student who avoids repetition entirely becomes incoherent. The useful condition lies between the two. There is, incidentally, a visual consequence to their anxiety. Students avoiding repetition often produce work that fractures into unrelated gestures: disconnected marks, unstable compositions, abrupt material shifts. What they describe as "multiplicity" is, more accurately, a refusal of continuity. The work does not develop. It disperses.

Unitas timetur. (Unity is feared.)

I once observed a student abandon a perfectly coherent series of drawings because they "felt too similar to each other." When pressed, they admitted that this similarity was the only element holding the work together. They then proceeded to begin a new series composed entirely of unrelated gestures, which they described, with admirable confidence, as "exploring multiplicity." The results were, predictably, incoherent–but vigorously defended. We must encourage this impulse, but only to a point. Coherence is not our enemy, but it is inconvenient. It creates patterns, and patterns allow students to infer rules. Once rules are inferred, they begin to believe they can be followed. Once they believe that, they begin to request guidance in writing. And once they request guidance in writing, we are already lost to administrative optimism. There is also an emerging tendency–one I find particularly tiresome–for students to "position" their work within broader artistic discourse. This is usually accompanied by diagrams, citations, and phrases such as "in conversation with." I have never once observed an actual conversation in these circumstances. At best, it is a series of polite monologues arranged in approximate proximity, each waiting for recognition from the other without risk of interruption.

Colloquium sine responsione. (Conversation without response.)

A minor but useful observation: students who obsess over originality rarely notice when they are imitating the *gesture* of originality itself. There is a particular tonal register they adopt–half caution, half declaration–which signals that they are attempting not to copy anyone, while carefully reproducing the structure of avoidance. We must not interrupt this too early. It is one of the more productive confusions available to us. However, we must also ensure that it does not resolve. Resolution produces identity. Identity produces stability. Stability produces the alarming suggestion that a student might be "developing a style." And once that phrase enters circulation, all other processes begin to slow, as though the system has mistaken repetition for completion. You may find it useful, therefore, to remind them–without emphasis–that originality is not a destination, but a misrecognition. Not of others, but of oneself.

Misrecognitio sui est principium motus. (Misrecognition of the self is the beginning of movement.)

And so, we arrive at the final distinction: They believe originality is something they must achieve. We understand it is something that is noticed–later, and by others. They avoid repetition in pursuit of difference. We preserve repetition as the condition from which difference occasionally emerges. A final note, included more for your amusement than instruction: The most "original" work in any cohort is almost always produced by students who were not attempting originality at all, but simply trying to finish something before the studio closed. We should not, under any circumstances, inform them of this. If we did, they would begin attempting not to try and that, paradoxically, would become another style.

Yours in managed imitation,

B. Judous

P.S
Is there a God?

12

Dear Mr Jaded Muse,

I am increasingly of the opinion that your students are no longer working in a studio at all, but in something closer to a carefully maintained theatre of artistic intention, in which the primary medium is not paint, clay, moving image, or sound, but the impression of becoming. This is not, strictly speaking, a complaint. The University has long encouraged a certain performative elasticity in its creative spaces. Studios have always been sites of observation as much as production–places where activity is not only undertaken, but witnessed, interpreted, and quietly evaluated. What concerns me is not that they are performing, but that they are beginning to believe the performance is incidental–something that happens *around* the work rather than *instead* of it.

Performatio fit natura. (Performance becomes nature.)

This, then, is the central misreading: That the appearance of practice is equivalent to its operation. You report that students are "presenting their process" with increasing seriousness. This phrase troubles me slightly, as it suggests they have mistaken visibility for substance. A process, once presented too frequently, ceases to function as a method of making and becomes a substitute for making itself. One begins to suspect that the work has not been delayed, but permanently replaced by its own description. From this misreading emerge several positions. The **reflective position** treats the articulation of process as evidence of development. To speak about the work is to understand it. Its strength lies in its clarity. Its weakness is that it confuses explanation with transformation. The **performative position** embraces visibility outright. The student does not merely make work; they enact the condition of making. Its strength is its immediacy. Its weakness is that it often produces gestures without consequence. The **institutional position**, predictably, rewards documentation and articulation as indicators of engagement. What can be shown, recorded, and described becomes legible—and therefore assessable. Its strength is its efficiency. Its weakness is that it quietly replaces production with evidence of production. Each position validates the presentation of practice. None ensures that practice is occurring. The matter, as ever, is structural. When process becomes visible too early, it ceases to function as process. A useful pedagogical observation: students who describe their work-in-progress aloud more than twice per session produce, on average, 39% fewer completed outcomes, but exhibit a 64% increase in confidence that they are "developing meaningfully." This is, of course, ideal. We have always preferred meaning that is perpetually in development rather than meaning that has arrived and begun asking inconvenient questions.

Melius fit quam fit. (Better to be becoming than to be.)

You will also have noticed the emergence of what I can only describe as a studio persona. This is the version of the student who enters the space slightly more decisive than the one who leaves it. The difference is usually accounted for by fatigue, peer observation, and a subtle fear that uncertainty might be mistaken for incompetence. It is remarkable how quickly they learn to behave like artists before becoming anything that might justify the behaviour. And yet, this persona is not merely imitation. It is defensive. It allows the student to occupy authorship before authorship has occurred, thereby reducing the risk of being seen in the act of not knowing.

Auctoritas praecocis. (Premature authorship.)

There is, however, a danger in allowing this theatricality to stabilise. A student who performs too convincingly eventually forgets they are performing at all. At that point, critique becomes particularly hazardous, as it is no longer received as guidance but as a disturbance in narrative continuity. I once observed a student respond to feedback not by disagreeing with it, but by stating, with considerable solemnity, “That is not how I experience my practice at this stage.” I confess I admired the phrasing even as I immediately adjusted their assessment downward for reasons I remain prepared to defend in writing, should institutional memory require clarification. We must also address their growing obsession with documentation. Everything is photographed, recorded, annotated, and occasionally narrated, as though the act of making were insufficient unless witnessed by a future that has not yet expressed interest. The studio is slowly becoming an archive of intentions rather than actions. A minor observation: students who document excessively develop a peculiar temporal confusion. They begin to believe that visibility is equivalent to completion. I have seen works achieve “resolution” in this way without ever achieving form–like a sentence declared finished before it has been spoken.

Visibile non est perfectum. (The visible is not the complete.)

At this point, one might be tempted to intervene–to reduce documentation, to discourage performance, to return the student to a more private and uncertain form of making. This would be premature. Here, the inversion becomes necessary. The theatre must remain. Performance, when allowed to extend, tends to collapse under its own sincerity. Students become so committed to presenting process that they forget to produce anything worth presenting. The performance consumes itself. This is instructive. You may also have noticed a new fashion for what students call "authentic presence" in the studio. This usually involves sitting beside unfinished work with a carefully calibrated expression of concern, occasionally moving a brush as if negotiating consent from the material itself. It is not without charm. It is also, unmistakably, performance. And yet–we must not remove it. A certain degree of self-misunderstanding is essential to the functioning of the department.

Sine errore, ars deficit. (Without error, art fails.)

There is, finally, the matter of observation itself. The most productive students are often those who have not yet realised they are being watched. The moment they become aware of the gaze–tutor, peer, institutional, they begin to curate themselves, and the work follows suit into polite ambiguity. This, I suspect, is the true condition of the contemporary studio: Not making, but being perceived making. And so, our task is not to remove the theatre, but to regulate its ambiguity. The performance must remain visible, but its status must remain uncertain. Students should never be entirely sure whether they are working, rehearsing, or presenting. For it is within this uncertainty that something–occasionally, and without warning–escapes performance altogether. Thus, the final distinction: They believe they are presenting their process. We understand they are performing its absence. They seek visibility as evidence of making. We preserve opacity as the condition under which making might occur. And so, the theatre continues–carefully staged, inconsistently believed, and rarely interrupted at the correct moment.

Incertus spectator, verus effectus. (An uncertain spectator produces the real effect.)

Yours in staged sincerity,

B. Judous

13

Dear Mr Jaded Muse,

It has come to my attention–through no deliberate inquiry on my part, but rather through the unfortunate habit students have of existing within audible range–that your cohort has begun to experience what they are pleased to call "uncertainty." The University, as you will have noticed, prefers to describe this condition in softer terms: "developmental ambiguity," "emergent thinking," or, on particularly optimistic days, "conceptual openness." These phrases are useful. They allow uncertainty to circulate without appearing as a failure of instruction, which would be considerably more difficult to justify in writing. This, then, is the central misreading: That uncertainty is a problem to be resolved. It is, I concede, an understandable belief. Uncertainty presents itself as absence of clarity, of direction, of meaning–and therefore appears to require completion. Students encounter it as a gap and assume it must be filled. They are mistaken. Uncertainty, properly maintained, is not a gap but a condition. Comparable, as you observe, to the moment in a studio critique when a student realises that charcoal does not, in fact, become oil paint through force of will alone. I have always found that one may measure artistic seriousness by the degree to which a student believes the medium is negotiable. It is not.

Medium non negotiabile est. (The medium is not negotiable.)

From this misreading emerge several positions. The **interpretive position** assumes that uncertainty arises from insufficient understanding. The student has not yet "found meaning," and must therefore search for it more effectively. Its strength lies in its persistence. Its weakness is that it treats meaning as discoverable rather than constructed. The **psychological position** frames uncertainty as insecurity–a lack of confidence that must be addressed through reassurance and support. Its strength is its compassion. Its weakness is that it often resolves uncertainty before it has had the opportunity to produce anything. The **institutional position**, predictably, treats uncertainty as a temporary phase. Students are expected to move through it toward clarity, coherence, and assessable outcomes. Its strength is its optimism. Its weakness is that it misunderstands duration. Each position seeks to reduce uncertainty. None understands its function. The matter, as ever, is structural. Uncertainty does not prevent work. It produces it. It enters, as you will have observed, with the theatrical inconvenience of a dropped sculpture, a misread brief, or a stretched canvas that refuses to sit correctly on its frame. Students begin to ask whether their work "means something," which is already the first sign that it does not yet mean enough. Meaning, as you know, is not an object one discovers, but a burden one persuades the work to carry without collapsing under its own interpretive weight.

A useful pedagogical fact for you here–file it under "minor truths best never cited in committee meetings": students are approximately 17% more likely to produce conceptual work after misplacing a piece of equipment they were emotionally dependent upon. This is not causation in any strict sense, but it behaves like it in exhibition contexts, which is often sufficient for institutional acceptance.

Desiderium instrumenti creat conceptum. (The loss of equipment creates concept.)

There is, incidentally, a visual analogue to this condition. Works produced under uncertainty tend to hover materially–unfinished joins, unresolved edges, surfaces that suggest intention without committing to it. The work neither resolves nor collapses; it simply hesitates in material form.

Hesitatio fit forma. (Hesitation becomes form.)

And yet–we must proceed carefully. There is a secondary misreading that emerges once uncertainty becomes familiar. Students begin to resolve it. They form what they call "artistic identities." This is always the moment at which they become least interesting and most insistent. Identity, in the undergraduate sense, is merely repetition with emotional emphasis and a carefully curated sense of internal continuity. It stabilises what should remain in motion. Here, then, the inversion becomes necessary. Uncertainty must be preserved–but not comfortably. Too much uncertainty produces paralysis: essays disguised as installations, statements in place of decisions, and a general reluctance to commit to anything that might later require explanation. Too little produces decorative certainty: clean edges, explanatory titles, and a worrying over-reliance on agreement. Between these lies the useful condition. A student should be uncertain–but functioning.

Certitudo decorativa est stabilitas falsa. (Decorative certainty is false stability.)

You may reassure them, if pressed, that no one in the history of serious artistic practice has ever benefited from being entirely sure of who they were. Even those we continue to cite–sometimes with more confidence than accuracy–appear, in retrospect, to have misunderstood themselves quite productively. Misunderstanding, in this sense, is not an error. It is a method. A further observation: students who begin to stabilise their identity prematurely tend to produce work that is consistent but unresponsive. They repeat decisions not because they are effective, but because they are recognisable. Recognition, once achieved, is rarely surrendered voluntarily. Consistency, in such cases, becomes a form of avoidance. You may find it useful, therefore, to resist any temptation to comfort them too efficiently. Comfort, pedagogically speaking, is a solvent. It dissolves ambition into opinion, and opinion into repetition with improved typography. That said, do not crush them entirely. I have attempted this approach myself during a particularly bleak autumn term and found that the resulting submissions resembled funerary pamphlets more than portfolios. We require a certain tension to remain intact–like a badly tuned instrument that nevertheless insists on performing in public. If you are uncertain how to calibrate this tension, I recommend the following rule, which I once derived while waiting for a departmental meeting that never occurred: A student should feel always slightly late for something they cannot name. This condition produces, with remarkable reliability, both anxiety and output in equal measure.

Tempus semper paulo praecurrit discipulum. (Time is always slightly ahead of the student.)

And so, we arrive at the final distinction: They believe uncertainty is something to be resolved. We understand it is something to be maintained. They seek clarity as evidence of progress. We preserve instability as the condition of movement. Uncertainty, after all, is not the enemy of creativity. It is its administrative assistant. It performs most of the paperwork. Our mistake, should we make one, would be to allow students to believe they are in control of either. You may tell them, if you wish, that clarity will come. This is not strictly untrue. It will arrive eventually–usually in the form of resignation dressed as maturity. Until then, keep them uncertain–but functioning.

Yours in managed ambiguity,

B. Judoug

14

Dear Mr Jaded Muse,

I am informed–though "informed" suggests a level of attentiveness I would not wish to claim–that your students have recently begun responding to encouragement. This is, naturally, alarming. The University has always maintained an ambiguous relationship with encouragement. It appears in feedback, hovers within critique, and occasionally settles into language that resembles approval. It is rarely examined directly. Like certain solvents kept in unlabelled containers, it is used frequently and understood poorly. This, then, is the central misreading: That encouragement is a form of support. It is, I concede, a tempting belief. Encouragement appears to stabilise the student, to increase confidence, and to produce a visible willingness to continue. These are all desirable outcomes–briefly. But such effects are rarely durable. Encouragement is one of those substances, like cheap varnish or unmoderated theory seminars, that initially appear to improve everything and then, with time, reveal themselves to have been actively dissolving the surface they were meant to protect. One applies it lightly, with optimism, and later discovers the entire structure has acquired the texture of damp cardboard and retrospective regret.

Confirmatio dissolvit structuram. (Affirmation dissolves structure.)

From this misreading emerge several positions. The

supportive position treats encouragement as essential nourishment. Students require validation in order to continue. Its strength lies in its compassion. Its weakness lies in its tendency to stabilise what should remain provisional. The **motivational position** frames encouragement as a stimulus. A well-timed affirmation increases productivity and reinforces positive behaviour. Its strength is its efficiency. Its weakness is that it often rewards appearance rather than substance. The **institutional position**, predictably, uses encouragement as a management tool. It regulates morale, maintains engagement, and reduces the visible symptoms of uncertainty. Its strength is its practicality. Its weakness is that it produces confidence without corresponding structure. Each position justifies encouragement. None accounts for its consequences. The matter, as ever, is structural. Encouragement does not support work. It stabilises interpretation. Students, for example, tend to interpret encouragement as confirmation rather than calibration. A slight nod in critique becomes, in their internal mythology, a coronation. What was intended as provisional becomes, in memory, decisive. I once observed a student transform the phrase "this has potential" into a three-year conceptual practice involving mirrors, regret, and what they described as "post-medium longing"–which, upon further inquiry, appeared to mean they had forgotten how to paint but wished this condition to be seen as theoretical. A small pedagogical observation for your consideration–one I share only because I suspect you will ignore it appropriately: students who receive encouragement within forty-eight hours of failure are approximately 23% more likely to misidentify failure as "a phase in their practice." This is technically accurate. It is also, in equal measure, emotionally catastrophic. At this point, one might be tempted to withdraw encouragement entirely. This would be unwise. Here, the inversion becomes necessary. Encouragement must remain–but only in altered form. We must refine it until it no longer resembles encouragement at all. It should not feel like approval. It should feel like conditional weather–present, shifting, and entirely uninterested in their interpretation of it. You may tell them, for instance, that they are "moving in an interesting direction." This phrase is invaluable. It contains no commitment, no praise, and no rescue. It merely implies movement exists, which is more than can be said for most of their ideas before midday.

Motus sine destinatione. (Movement without destination.)

Equally useful is the expression: "There is something here." This is not a sentence; it is a corridor. Students will spend years walking down it, assuming it leads somewhere other than itself, occasionally mistaking repetition for arrival. There is, however, a further complication. Encouragement interacts unpredictably with identity. You may have encountered the increasingly fashionable instruction to "trust your voice." I would advise caution. I have listened closely to the average student voice. It is not a voice. It is a committee meeting conducted in a corridor with poor acoustics and excessive self-reference.

Vox non una, sed collectio. (Not one voice, but a collection.)

Trust, in this context, becomes a form of abandonment. One does not encourage a student to trust their voice any

more than one encourages an untrained instrument to trust its own tuning. Instead, we should cultivate hesitation–though never name it as such. Hesitation, when properly disguised as reflection, produces far more reliable output. It slows certainty, interrupts premature conclusions, and prevents the formation of style before structure has had the opportunity to emerge. And yet, as always, there is a limit.
If encouragement is entirely withheld, students begin to believe we are hostile. Some are correct, but this is not pedagogically useful information. Others respond with work of such defensive intensity that it resembles architectural revenge–structures built not to be inhabited, but to withstand imagined critique. We must therefore maintain a delicate equilibrium: Enough encouragement to sustain production. Not enough to allow them to conclude they are finished.

Stabilitas approbationis periculosa est. (Stability of approval is dangerous.)

A further observation: students who receive consistent encouragement tend to produce work that is increasingly stable, increasingly legible, and increasingly resistant to change. Stability, in this sense, is not achievement but stagnation with institutional approval. Occasionally, I have found it useful to praise a student in such a way that they become slightly suspicious of their own success. This is not cruelty. It is hygiene. Encouragement, like all effective pedagogical instruments, is best used indirectly. It should not be delivered. It should be inferred. The student should leave the room uncertain whether they have been praised, corrected, or quietly dismissed. This ambiguity is not a failure of communication. It is its condition. Thus, the final distinction: They believe encouragement confirms their progress. We understand it destabilises their certainty. They seek approval as evidence of arrival. We provide ambiguity as a condition of continuation. If they are ever certain, we have failed them.

Yours in calibrated ambiguity,

B. Judous

15

Dear Mr Jaded Muse,

I am beginning to suspect that your students have developed what can only be described as certainty without evidence. This is, as you will appreciate, one of the more fashionable afflictions of the present academic climate–particularly in art departments, where conviction is frequently mistaken for competence and posture for process. The institution, for its part, does little to discourage this condition. Certainty is efficient. It presents well in assessment environments, reduces hesitation in critique, and produces statements that can be archived without requiring excessive interpretation. It is, in short, administratively convenient. This, then, is the central misreading: That certainty is a sign of understanding. It is, I concede, an appealing assumption. Certainty has the appearance of clarity. It speaks fluently, occupies space confidently, and resists interruption. Students who exhibit it are often mistaken for those who have "arrived," though one is rarely certain where. They now speak, I am told, with increasing confidence about "their practice." I always find this phrasing revealing. A practice, properly understood, is not something one possesses but something that occurs to one over time, often inconveniently and without consent. Students, however, have begun to treat it as a possession–like a particularly stubborn coat or an inherited chair that cannot be disposed of without symbolic guilt.

Praxis non habetur, sed patitur. (Practice is not held, but endured.)

From this misreading emerge several positions. The **expressive position** treats certainty as authenticity. If the student feels certain, then the work must be true to them. Its strength lies in its immediacy. Its weakness lies in its indifference to structure. The **professional position** treats certainty as confidence–a necessary quality for survival within the art world. Its strength is its pragmatism. Its weakness is that it often produces performance without substance. The **institutional position**, predictably, treats certainty as progress. A student who speaks clearly about their work is assumed to understand it. Its strength is its legibility. Its weakness is that it confuses articulation with comprehension. Each position reinforces certainty. None interrogates it. The matter, as ever, is structural. Certainty does not emerge from understanding. It replaces it. A small pedagogical fact I must share with you–though I warn you it is unsuitable for polite funding documentation: students who describe their work as “my practice” within their first term are statistically 31% more likely to abandon making in favour of describing making. This is not a failure in the conventional sense. It is something more refined: The successful reclassification of inactivity as identity. At this point, the student is no longer uncertain about the work. They are certain about the idea of having work. The distinction is subtle but operationally significant. You will also notice that certainty produces a peculiar aesthetic effect in their work: It hardens it. The work begins to resemble declaration rather than exploration. Surfaces become fixed, decisions appear pre-justified, and even failure acquires a curatorial tone–as though disappointment has been pre-authorised and formatted in advance.

Certitudo forma clauditur. (Certainty closes form.)

It would be tempting, at this stage, to correct the student–to introduce doubt, to destabilise their claims, to remind them of the provisional nature of their position. This would be inefficient. Here, the inversion becomes necessary. Certainty should not be removed. It should be redirected. One of the more effective methods I have found is to allow their certainty to expand until it becomes visibly cumbersome. Certainty, left unattended, has a natural tendency toward inflation. It becomes increasingly difficult for the student to carry into critique spaces without colliding with other people's uncertainty. At that point, intervention is no longer required. Gravity performs the correction. There is also a diagnostic dimension worth noting. Students exhibiting early certainty are approximately 46% more likely to produce work that explains itself before it exists. Titles precede images, statements anticipate outcomes, and language arrives fully formed while the work remains tentative. This reversal of sequence is not accidental; it is structural. Explanation stabilises what has not yet occurred. A further observation for your records: certainty in first-year students correlates strongly with an inability to distinguish critique from weather. They will interpret "this is unclear" as a meteorological condition affecting their identity rather than their work. This misunderstanding is, I admit, occasionally more productive than clarity. You must resist the temptation to correct certainty too directly. Direct correction produces resistance. Resistance produces manifestos. And manifestos, as you know, require both wall space and institutional apology procedures. Instead, allow doubt to enter quietly, as though it has not yet decided whether it belongs there. A well-placed question, left unresolved, is usually sufficient. The student will then proceed to fill the silence with increasingly elaborate interpretations of their own uncertainty. This is ideal. And yet, as always, there is a limit. A student without certainty produces only atmospheric uncertainty–work that hovers without commitment, language that dissolves upon contact, and decisions that defer themselves indefinitely. This condition is indistinguishable from fog and equally resistant to assessment. We must therefore maintain a precise imbalance. Not certainty. No doubt. But misalignment between the two. What we require is misplaced certainty: Certainty directed at the wrong aspect of the work. Let them be absolutely convinced of intention while remaining entirely incorrect about its manifestation. Let them defend decisions they have not yet made and explain structures that do not yet exist. This combination yields the most reliable exhibition material.

Certitudo errans fructifera est. (Misplaced certainty is productive.)

There is, incidentally, a final distinction worth preserving:n They believe certainty confirms their understanding. We understand it conceals their uncertainty. They seek to stabilise their position. We allow it to destabilise itself. I trust you will continue your efforts in this regard, ideally without fully understanding why they succeed. That, in my experience, remains the most stable foundation for pedagogy.

Yours in structured misapprehension,

B. Judous

P.S. Did you say there was a God?

16

Dear Mr Jaded Muse,

It has come to my attention–via the usual channels of academic rumour, complaint, and a student who mistook me for someone willing to listen–that your cohort is beginning to experience disappointment in significant quantities. This is, I assure you, entirely appropriate. The University has always maintained a productive relationship with disappointment. It circulates quietly through studios, accumulates during critique, and settles most comfortably in the space between intention and outcome. It is rarely acknowledged directly, though it is almost always present. This, then, is the central misreading: That disappointment is a failure of progress. It is, I concede, an understandable conclusion. Disappointment presents itself as absence of success, of recognition, of completion, and therefore appears to indicate that something has gone wrong. Students, encountering it for the first time in sufficient concentration, assume it must be corrected. They are mistaken. Disappointment, when correctly administered, is not a failure of teaching but its most reliable by-product. One might even argue that the University exists primarily as a carefully regulated apparatus for the distribution of disappointment–though I would hesitate to state this anywhere more permanent than a private letter to you, and even then only because I assume you will misplace it. Your students, I am told, are disappointed in their work, in each other, and–most promisingly–in the general existence of time as a limiting condition. This last category is particularly fertile. A student who discovers that time does not bend to their conceptual framework is, at last, approaching something resembling education.

Disappointatio est forma cognitionis non resoluta. (Disappointment is a form of unresolved cognition.)

From this misreading emerge several positions. The **emotional position** treats disappointment as discouragement—a state to be alleviated through reassurance and support. Its strength lies in its immediacy. Its weakness lies in its tendency to remove the very condition that produces reflection. The **developmental position** frames disappointment as a stage—temporary, transitional, and ultimately resolvable. Its strength is its optimism. Its weakness is that it encourages premature resolution. The **institutional position**, predictably, treats disappointment as a risk factor. Too much of it produces withdrawal; too little produces complacency. Its strength is its caution. Its weakness is that it misunderstands intensity. Each position attempts to manage disappointment. None understands its function. The matter, as ever, is structural. Disappointment does not interrupt learning. It exposes the distance between expectation and operation. It is, in this sense, diagnostic. A small pedagogical observation, for your private amusement: students who experience disappointment before noon are approximately 18% more likely to produce work they later describe as "authentic," regardless of its actual content. Authenticity, of course, is the term we reserve for states of making that have not yet been subjected to successful evaluation. At this stage, one might be tempted to reduce disappointment—to soften its edges, to reframe its implications, to reassure the student that they are "on the right track." This would be inefficient. Here, the inversion becomes necessary. Disappointment must not be removed. It must be maintained in motion. We must avoid, at all costs, its resolution into resignation. Resignation is a quiet ending, and quiet endings are dangerous in art departments, as they frequently result in submissions that are both complete and entirely without consequence. What we require instead is active disappointment: Disappointment that continues to move. Disappointment that resists closure. Disappointment that remains slightly offended by its own persistence. A student should feel, at all times, that something almost worked, but has deliberately chosen not to complete itself. You will observe that students are particularly vulnerable to disappointment when they begin comparing themselves to one another. Comparison, in this regard, is one of the most efficient teaching assistants available to us. It requires no salary, no recognition, and produces immediate instability across otherwise manageable cohorts. I once attempted to eliminate comparison entirely from a group, purely as an experiment. The result was catastrophic. The students became calm, collaborative, and briefly competent. Fortunately, this condition proved unsustainable. They soon rediscovered social media, and normal pedagogical entropy resumed. We should therefore encourage comparison–but never allow clarity about its object. Let them compare outcomes without understanding methods. Ambition without understanding discipline. Confidence without understanding cost. This produces a particularly productive form of disappointment: one that believes itself to be the result of injustice rather than preparation.

Disparitas sine causa perspicua fertilis est. (Disparity without clear cause is fertile.)

There is, I think, a deeper principle here worth stating–though I do so reluctantly, as it risks sounding like philosophy rather than administration: Disappointment only becomes useful when it is misattributed. If a student correctly understands the source of their disappointment, they begin to adjust. We cannot permit this too early. Better that they believe the fault lies in timing, environment, peers, funding structures, weather, dietary choices, or the metaphysical indifference of the University itself. Any explanation will do– Provided it is not accurate. There is also a recognisable aesthetic register to disappointment. Works produced under its influence tend toward muted tones, unresolved forms, and titles that resemble apologies written under duress. The surface hesitates. The composition withdraws. The work appears to apologise for its own existence while insisting on being seen. This is excellent. It indicates that disappointment has reached the correct depth without yet stabilising into reflection. A further observation: students experiencing sustained disappointment are approximately 49% more likely to revise their language before revising their work. Statements become more complex, more defensive, and more abstract –while the work itself remains materially unchanged. Language, in this context, performs compensatory labour.

We must allow this–but not mistake it for progress. And yet, as always, there is a limit. Excessive disappointment produces collapse: withdrawal, silence, and the gradual disappearance of work altogether. This is not useful. A student who ceases to produce ceases to participate, and participation, as you know, need not be genuine to be effective. We must therefore maintain a precise calibration: Enough disappointment to destabilise expectation. Not enough to eliminate production. Thus, the final distinction: They believe disappointment indicates failure. We understand it produces recognition. They seek to resolve it. We ensure it continues. A student prematurely relieved of disappointment becomes dangerously coherent. And coherence, in early artistic development, is either a sign of brilliance or administrative error. We should assume the latter until proven otherwise. In conclusion, I urge you to continue your careful stewardship of their dissatisfaction. It is one of the few abundant resources remaining in contemporary education, and we would be unwise not to extract it with appropriate discipline.

Yours in calibrated discouragement,

B. Judous

17

Dear Mr Jaded Muse,

It has come to my attention–though I should clarify that "attention" is here used in the same sense as a man glancing at a storm while pretending it is a curtain–that your students are once again misunderstanding almost everything. I must reassure you immediately: This is not only acceptable, but actively desirable. The University, when operating at its most effective, does not produce understanding in any stable or transferable sense. It produces conditions in which understanding appears intermittently, often by accident, and rarely in the form in which it was requested. To aim for clarity directly would be to mistake education for instruction, which, as you know, is a considerably narrower and less interesting activity. This, then, is the central misreading: That misunderstanding is an error to be corrected. It is, I concede, a compelling belief. Misunderstanding presents itself as deviation–a failure to grasp intention, instruction, or meaning–and therefore appears to require correction. Students, encountering it repeatedly, assume they are doing something wrong. They are not. A University of Creative Studies, properly functioning, should resemble a large and carefully supervised misunderstanding with occasional moments of accidental clarity. Too much clarity produces essays; too much misunderstanding produces funding concerns. We must therefore maintain the delicate middle condition: Students should be almost correct often enough to persist, but never correct enough to relax into competence.

Inter intellectum et errorem stat ars. (Art stands between understanding and error.)

From this misreading emerge several positions. The **corrective position** treats misunderstanding as deficiency. The student has failed to comprehend and must therefore be guided more clearly. Its strength lies in its precision. Its weakness lies in its tendency to eliminate the very conditions under which discovery occurs. The **interpretive position** reframes misunderstanding as alternative meaning. The student has not misunderstood, but reinterpreted. Its strength is its generosity. Its weakness is that it risks validating incoherence as insight. The **institutional position**, predictably, oscillates between the two. It corrects where necessary and celebrates where convenient. Its strength is its flexibility. Its weakness is that it has no stable criteria for either. Each position attempts to manage misunderstanding. None understands its function.

The matter, as ever, is structural. Misunderstanding does not obstruct learning. It produces variation. A small pedagogical observation for your consideration: students who consistently misunderstand critique are approximately 27% more likely to develop what they call a "distinctive voice," which, upon closer inspection, usually means they have repeated the same interpretive error with increasing confidence and improved punctuation. This is not without value. Repetition stabilises error. Stabilised error becomes style. You may have noticed that misunderstanding has a peculiar behavioural effect. It produces enthusiasm without direction, conviction without foundation, and collaboration without agreement. In other words, it produces precisely what exhibition catalogues tend to describe–without irony –as "dynamic tension." We must not interfere with this too aggressively. Misunderstanding is one of the few self-renewing resources available to us. It replenishes itself every time a student encounters feedback and decides, quite reasonably from their position, that it refers to someone else entirely. I have often observed that students do not so much misinterpret instruction as re-route it. A critique intended to address composition becomes, in their internal translation system, a comment on biography, temperament, or atmospheric pressure. A suggestion about material becomes an inquiry into identity. A question becomes a position. This is not failure. It is adaptive creativity under constraint.

Interpretatio est deformis sed fertilis. (Misinterpretation is distorted but fertile.)

And yet, as always, there is a limit. Misunderstanding, if left entirely unchecked, occasionally resolves into unintended insight. A student may, by accident or exhaustion, grasp what was meant. This is always regrettable. And usually requires immediate soft correction through further ambiguity. Here, the inversion becomes necessary. Misunderstanding must not be eliminated. It must be regulated. We must maintain a controlled instability in all instructional language. Not enough to induce panic, but sufficient to ensure that meaning never settles comfortably in one place. A sentence should behave like a guest who has not yet decided whether to leave or to remain indefinitely out of politeness. This produces a particular kind of attentiveness–one that does not rely on comprehension, but on proximity to meaning. There is also the matter of peer-to-peer misunderstanding, which is even more valuable. When students misunderstand one another, they begin to construct what they believe are shared positions. These positions are, in fact, parallel solitudes temporarily mistaken for consensus. This is ideal. It prevents the dangerous emergence of actual agreement.

Consensus est error approbatus. (Consensus is approved error.)

You may find it useful to encourage group critique sessions in which no one is entirely certain whether they are agreeing, disagreeing, or simply continuing previous sentences spoken by other people. This produces excellent outcomes: Heightened emotional investment. Occasional rupture. And work that becomes progressively harder to describe in assessment meetings without resorting to metaphorical evacuation. A further observation: students who misunderstand each other consistently are approximately 34% more likely to produce collaborative work that appears conceptually dense but structurally indeterminate. This is particularly useful in exhibition contexts, where density often substitutes for coherence. We must, however, avoid one critical error: Correction. A corrected misunderstanding becomes understanding. Understanding tends toward closure. Closure is aesthetically terminal. It is far better to allow misunderstanding to mature. Left alone, it develops texture, internal justification, and a strong tendency to present itself as reflection in written work. At this stage, it becomes indistinguishable from intention. And intention, as you know, is rarely questioned once properly phrased.

Thus, the final distinction: They believe misunderstanding is a failure to be corrected. We understand it is a condition to be sustained. They seek clarity as resolution. We maintain ambiguity as operation. We are not, after all, in the business of clarity. We are in the business of productive confusion under supervision.

Yours in structured misapprehension,

B. Judous

18

Dear Mr Jaded Muse,

It has been brought to my attention–by which I mean I overheard it through the thin partition of a corridor while pretending to examine a noticeboard–that you have once again been praising your students. This is, I regret to inform you, an act that requires far more precision than you are currently demonstrating. The University, as you will have observed, maintains an ambiguous relationship with praise. It appears in feedback, circulates through critique, and occasionally settles into language that resembles approval. It is rarely examined as an instrument, though it is deployed with remarkable frequency. This, then, is the central misreading: That praise is a reward. It is, I concede, a convenient belief. Praise appears to acknowledge success, reinforce effort, and stabilise confidence. Students receive it as confirmation; staff distribute it as encouragement; the institution records it as progress. All parties benefit– Briefly. But such benefits are rarely structural. Praise, in the context of our University of Creative Studies, is not a reward. It is a calibrated instrument, comparable to a chisel that occasionally forgets it is not a hammer. In inexperienced hands, it produces sculpture; in student hands, it produces certainty, which is a far more brittle and therefore more dangerous material.

Praemium sine tensione est corruptio. (Reward without tension is corruption.)

From this misreading emerge several positions. The **affirmative position** treats praise as necessary support. Students require recognition in order to continue. Its strength lies in its generosity. Its weakness lies in its tendency to stabilise premature conclusions. The **motivational position** frames praise as incentive. Positive reinforcement encourages further production. Its strength is its efficiency. Its weakness is that it often rewards appearance rather than structure. The **institutional position**, predictably, treats praise as documentation. It provides evidence of engagement, development, and success. Its strength is its legibility. Its weakness is that it confuses approval with advancement. Each position distributes praise. None regulates its effect. The matter, as ever, is structural. Praise does not improve work. It arrests movement. A small pedagogical observation for your records: students who receive unqualified praise are approximately 34% more likely to misinterpret uncertainty as failure and failure as identity. This is not strictly their fault. It is, as so much in education is, a design feature that has acquired the tone of moral discourse. You will observe that praise has a peculiar effect on the student's perceptual system. It does not encourage improvement so much as it stabilises interpretation. The student begins to behave as though they have already arrived, which is a particularly unfortunate condition for anyone still physically enrolled in a programme defined by continuous instability. I have seen entire cohorts transform, within a single week of excessive praise, into small monuments of premature completion. They sit in studios like finished ideas waiting for applause that has already been misallocated elsewhere. At this point, one might be tempted to withdraw praise entirely. This would be an error. Here, the inversion becomes necessary.

Praise must not be removed. It must be destabilised. We must return it to its proper function: Not affirmation, but disturbance. A properly administered compliment should leave the student slightly unsettled. If they are comfortable after receiving it, you have not applied it correctly. For example, rather than saying "this is strong work," one might say: "This is strong work, which is surprising given your usual tendency toward decorative uncertainty." This produces a productive imbalance. The student is now uncertain whether they have improved or merely been temporarily tolerated. This ambiguity is, of course, the desired condition.

Stabilitas laudis est periculum cognitionis. (Stability of praise is a danger to understanding.)

You may object that such methods risk discouraging students. This is correct. They are, after all, students. Discouragement is not a malfunction in their system; it is one of its primary operational states. What we must avoid at all costs is stabilised self-esteem. Once a student believes their value is consistent, they cease to behave as material and begin to behave as authority. And authority, in an undergraduate context, is always premature and therefore aesthetically unconvincing. There is also the matter of peer amplification. Students do not merely receive praise; they circulate it, reinterpret it, and return it to one another in progressively inflated form. What begins as "an interesting idea" becomes, by the third retelling, "a decisive intervention in contemporary visual language." This inflation must be managed carefully. Otherwise, we find ourselves producing not artists, but small economies of mutual reassurance operating under the illusion of critique.

I once attempted to allow praise to circulate freely without moderation. The result was catastrophic. Within three weeks, every student believed they were "on a trajectory." No one could specify toward what, but the confidence was extraordinary. The work, however, resembled packaging for something that had not yet been invented. A further observation: students who receive consistent praise are approximately 41% more likely to repeat successful gestures rather than develop them. Repetition, in this context, is not exploration but preservation. We must therefore ensure that praise always carries a faint residue of doubt. Not enough to destabilise production entirely, but sufficient to prevent students from mistaking approval for completion.
Think of praise as salt in a complex dish: Too little, and nothing develops. Too much, and preservation replaces transformation. And above all, do not allow praise to become kindness. Kindness is not pedagogically neutral; it is structurally permissive. It invites students to remain as they are, which is the one condition we cannot afford to stabilise.

Consensio sine frictione est stasis. (Agreement without friction is stasis.)

Thus, the final distinction: They believe praise confirms their value. We understand it destabilises their position. They seek approval as evidence of progress. We provide ambiguity as a condition of continuation. I trust you will adjust your practice accordingly, or at least continue to disguise your instincts with sufficient ambiguity to remain institutionally defensible.

Yours in carefully rationed approval,

B. Judous

P.S.

I now believe in the one. Are any churches open anymore??

19

Dear Mr Jaded Muse,

It has become increasingly apparent–through the usual combination of student complaints, departmental gossip, and a misplaced portfolio left open in a corridor–that your current understanding of "talent" is dangerously unrefined. I should clarify at once that talent, in the context of our University of Creative Studies, is not a virtue. It is a raw material with a distressing tendency to misbehave when acknowledged too directly. The institution, as you will have observed, maintains a conflicted relationship with it. Talent is identified, celebrated, and occasionally displayed–though rarely understood. It is praised in language that suggests stability, while behaving in ways that resist it entirely. This, then, is the central misreading: That talent is an indicator of direction. It is, I concede, an attractive assumption. Talent appears to point somewhere. It suggests potential, implies trajectory, and reassures both student and tutor that progress is not only possible, but already underway. Students, upon recognising it in themselves–or having it recognised for them–begin to organise their behaviour accordingly. They are mistaken.

Talentum non est virtus, sed perturbatio. (Talent is not virtue, but disturbance.)

From this misreading emerge several positions. The **developmental position** treats talent as a resource to be nurtured. It must be supported, guided, and encouraged toward fulfilment. Its strength lies in its optimism. Its weakness lies in its tendency to stabilise what should remain unstable. The **evaluative position** treats talent as a marker of distinction. It identifies those who are "ahead" and structures attention accordingly. Its strength is its efficiency. Its weakness is that it confuses visibility with substance. The **institutional position**, predictably, treats talent as an asset. It is highlighted, promoted, and occasionally instrumentalised for the purposes of reputation. Its strength is its utility. Its weakness is that it converts uncertainty into expectation. Each position attempts to secure talent. None understands its behaviour. The matter, as ever, is structural. Talent does not indicate where a student is going. It destabilises where they are. A small pedagogical observation for your files: students labelled as "talented" in their first year are approximately 41% more likely to develop an incurable dependency on early praise and lukewarm coffee. Neither condition is easily corrected, and both tend to masquerade as artistic temperament. At this stage, talent begins to shift function. It is no longer a capacity. It becomes an explanation. The student ceases to ask what the work is doing and begins to assume it must be doing something significant, simply because they are doing it. You will have noticed, I trust, that students designated as talented often begin to behave as though the work is already complete. Their output becomes anticipatory–sketches of conclusions rather than propositions under construction, declarations of intent rather than acts of sustained making. One might say they begin to produce results in advance of having done anything. This is not progress. It is aesthetic prepayment.

Ante actum conclusio est defectus formae. (A conclusion before action is a failure of form.)

At this point, one might be tempted to intervene–to challenge the student, to destabilise their confidence, to reintroduce doubt. This would be insufficient. Here, the inversion becomes necessary. Talent must not be reinforced. It must be displaced. We must ensure that talent is never allowed to remain properly located. It should always feel slightly misplaced–issued the wrong key, for the wrong studio, at the wrong stage of development. Certainty about talent is its most dangerous condition. Uncertainty is its only useful one. There is also a secondary danger you must attend to: Talent attracts interpretation. The more talented a student is believed to be, the more others project coherence onto their work, until eventually the student is no longer producing art but responding to a collective hallucination of significance. This is particularly visible in group critiques, where "genius" is frequently deployed as a substitute for sustained looking. The work becomes insulated by language. And language, once stabilised, is rarely challenged. We must resist this tendency. Genius, as far as I can determine, is simply talent that has not yet been interrupted often enough to become self-satisfied.

Interruptio est forma tutelae. (Interruption is a form of protection.)

A further observation: students consistently identified as talented are approximately 38% more likely to avoid situations in which their work might visibly fail. They gravitate toward conditions that confirm their ability and withdraw from those that might expose its limits. This produces a particular aesthetic condition: Work that is fluent but cautious. Competent but untested. Convincing but curiously uncommitted. We must not allow this to stabilise. Talent, when protected, becomes decorative competence. And decorative competence is indistinguishable from completion. There is, however, a more subtle complication. Some students do possess genuine capacity. It is rarely where they believe it to be. It appears most often in their failures, their hesitations, and the occasional accidental honesty that emerges when they are too tired to perform ambition correctly. These moments are easily overlooked. Or worse– Misidentified as exceptions. It is our task–not an especially pleasant one–to ensure that they do not mistake these moments for conclusions.

We must also resist the increasingly institutional habit of protecting talent from difficulty. This is a particularly modern form of negligence. It produces students exquisitely skilled at avoiding the very conditions under which skill might become visible. We must instead expose talent to resistance. Not enough to destroy it. But sufficient to ensure it remains aware of its own limitations. Without resistance, talent does not develop. It accumulates.
And accumulation, as you know, is rarely transformative. Thus, the final distinction: They believe talent indicates what they are capable of. We understand it obscures what they have not yet encountered. They seek to stabilise it as identity. We destabilise it as condition. Talent, after all, is not rare. What is rare is talent that survives contact with time, critique, misunderstanding, and the mildly absurd expectations of the art world without becoming either resentful or self-congratulatory. Our role is not to preserve talent, but to prevent it from mistaking itself for achievement.

Yours in calibrated disregard,

B. Judous

20

Dear Mr Jaded Muse,

It has come to my attention–through the usual unreliable triangulation of student feedback, overheard studio conversations, and a critique sheet left fluttering like a guilty bird on my desk–that your students are beginning to believe they are independent. This is, I must say, one of the more charming delusions of early artistic training, comparable only to the belief that a badly stretched canvas is a statement rather than a material oversight. The University, as you will have noticed, encourages this belief in subtle and carefully deniable ways. We speak of autonomy, self-direction, and independent practice, while quietly arranging the conditions under which these can be performed without ever fully occurring. This, then, is the central misreading: That independence is a condition the student can achieve. It is, I concede, a persuasive idea. Independence suggests maturity, authorship, and a form of intellectual self-sufficiency that is both admirable and administratively convenient. Students, upon encountering it, begin to organise themselves accordingly. They speak differently. They decide differently. They perform certainty with increasing fluency. They are mistaken. Independence, in the student sense, is rarely independence at all. It is simply dependency that has misplaced its origin.

Independencia est ignorantia relationis. (Independence is ignorance of relation.)

From this misreading emerge several positions. The **developmental position** treats independence as a goal. The student must gradually detach from instruction and assume responsibility for their own work. Its strength lies in its clarity. Its weakness lies in its naivety. The **expressive position** frames independence as authenticity. The student must find their own voice, their own direction, their own system of meaning. Its strength is its appeal. Its weakness is that it often replaces structure with declaration. The **institutional position**, predictably, treats independence as evidence. A student who appears self-directed is assumed to be progressing. Its strength is its efficiency. Its weakness is that it confuses performance with condition.

Each position promotes independence. None accounts for its construction. The matter, as ever, is structural. Independence does not emerge from the absence of influence. It emerges from the misrecognition of it. A small pedagogical observation for your records: students who believe they are working independently are approximately 29% more likely to seek approval in increasingly indirect and aesthetically elaborate forms, including–but not limited to–what they call "conceptual ambiguity." This is, of course, entirely expected. Approval, once displaced, does not disappear. It reappears. Diffused, aestheticised, and more difficult to identify. You will observe that students in this condition begin to externalise judgment. They no longer ask "Is this good?" but rather "Would this be seen as good?" This is not a refinement. It is a relocation. Authority has not been removed. It has been redistributed. At this point, one might be tempted to intervene–to reveal the dependency, to clarify the structure, to restore a more honest relationship between student and system. This would be inefficient. Here, the inversion becomes necessary. Independence must not be dismantled. It must be maintained as illusion. We must ensure that independence remains decorative rather than functional. Allow them to speak of autonomy freely. It costs us nothing, and it provides them with the reassuring sensation of self-direction. Meanwhile, we continue to shape the conditions under which any meaningful decision can occur. This is not manipulation. It is curriculum design with improved narrative framing. There is a principle here worth stating plainly: The most effective dependency is the one the student believes they have chosen. This is not difficult to achieve. One simply ensures that all available choices are arranged such that refusal resembles negligence, and acceptance resembles insight.

Eligere sine fuga est forma obedientiae. (Choice without escape is a form of obedience.)

A further observation: students placed in environments of structured freedom produce approximately 37% more "personal work" and 52% more uncertainty regarding what "personal" signifies. This is, again, entirely satisfactory. The work appears self-directed. The student remains structurally dependent. You will also note that independence produces a recognisable aesthetic register: Fragmentation. Hesitation disguised as conceptual depth. Titles that read like apologies filtered through translation errors and group consensus. These are not signs of autonomy. They are indicators of unacknowledged structure. We must not correct this too quickly. These are early symptoms of productive dependency. If resolved prematurely, they collapse into clarity– And clarity, as you know, is simply dependency that has escaped supervision and begun misidentifying itself as resolution. There is also the matter of peer reinforcement. Students will validate one another's independence with extraordinary enthusiasm, particularly when none of them are actually independent. This collective performance of autonomy is one of our most valuable resources. It creates the appearance of self-direction while ensuring that all decisions remain socially administered. I once observed a cohort describe themselves as "self-sustaining." Within three weeks, they were unable to initiate a project without a group discussion, a shared document, and at least one existential crisis reframed as methodology. We should aim to preserve this condition. A final observation: students who believe themselves independent are approximately 42% more resistant to direct instruction, but 63% more responsive to indirect influence. This asymmetry is of considerable practical value and should not be disrupted unnecessarily. And yet, as always, there is a limit. A student who becomes genuinely independent will, for a brief and unsettling period, begin to resemble an artist. This is inefficient, difficult to assess, and resistant to categorisation in moderation meetings. We must avoid it. Thus, the final distinction: They believe independence is the absence of influence. We understand it is the misrecognition of it. They seek autonomy as condition. We provide it as appearance. Much better to maintain the gentle fiction that autonomy is always imminent but never achieved–while ensuring that every apparent step toward it increases their reliance on the conditions that produce it. In this way, we preserve both movement and dependence, which is to say: The ideal educational state.

Yours in carefully distributed influence,

B. Judous

PS. Our church got hit by lightning. Do you think this is a sign?

21

Dear Mr Jaded Muse,

It has become necessary–again–to address what I can only describe as your students' increasing comfort. I note this not with alarm, precisely, but with a kind of institutional unease that tends to arise whenever a system designed for instability begins to resemble something like equilibrium. Comfort, in such environments, is rarely accidental. It accumulates quietly, settles into routines, and eventually presents itself as progress. This, as you will have already begun to suspect, is not progress. Comfort, as you will have discovered if you have spent more than a fortnight in a studio critique, is rarely the ally of artistic development. It behaves instead like a well-meaning relative at a funeral: present, persistent, and quietly obstructing anything resembling transformation. Your students, I am told, are beginning to settle. They arrive on time, prepare work in advance, and speak in measured tones about "process". All of this is extremely worrying. They have mistaken continuity for movement. Or more precisely: They have mistaken the absence of disruption for the presence of development. It is, I concede, a plausible confusion. From one perspective–the **procedural**, if we must name it–comfort appears efficient. Work is produced regularly, discussions are coherent, and the studio begins to resemble a space in which things happen in an orderly fashion. Its strength lies in its visibility. Its weakness is that nothing actually changes. The **psychological position**, more forgiving, frames comfort as safety. Students require stability in order to explore. Its strength is its compassion. Its weakness is that exploration conducted without resistance tends to produce confirmation rather than discovery. The **institutional position**, as ever, is conflicted. Comfort produces compliance, and compliance produces legible outcomes. These are not negligible benefits. But they arrive at a cost that is rarely accounted for: The disappearance of risk. And with it– The disappearance of necessity. A student who is settled is a student who has mistaken continuity for progress. A small pedagogical observation for your records: students reporting high levels of comfort in studio environments are approximately 44% more likely to produce work that resembles interior design by accident. This is not a judgment. It is merely a description of form under reduced pressure. Surfaces stabilise. Decisions become polite. Colours agree with one another in ways that suggest negotiation rather than necessity. The work ceases to argue. And when the work ceases to argue, It ceases to require attention. We must therefore reintroduce a controlled degree of anxiety. Not chaos–chaos produces administration–but something quieter, more continuous: A distributed sense of inadequacy. Not assigned. Not explained. Simply present.

Anxietas non est perturbatio, sed motus continuus. (Anxiety is not disturbance, but continuous motion.)

You will observe that anxiety, unlike comfort, produces motion. It interrupts certainty. It disturbs self-congratulation. It introduces the possibility–however unwelcome–that the last decision was insufficient. This is, in many respects, the beginning of revision. But it must be handled with care. Too much anxiety produces paralysis. Too little produces portfolios that believe they are already complete. We require the narrow corridor between these states– The corridor in which students are always slightly regretting what they have just done, while remaining unsure how to improve it. It is in this interval that work begins to move. There is, however, a further complication. Anxiety behaves socially. It does not distribute itself evenly. One student's doubt becomes another's temporary confidence, which then collapses upon contact with critique, producing a continuous exchange of instability across the cohort. This is, in effect, our unofficial pedagogy. We must not interfere with this cycle unless it becomes too coherent. Coherence, in groups, is rarely a sign of understanding. It is more often a sign that anxiety has settled into agreement. And agreement, as you know, is simply anxiety that has agreed with itself, and therefore ceased to function. A further observation: students exposed to ambient uncertainty for sustained periods develop a measurable increase in what they describe as "artistic seriousness," which usually manifests as longer studio hours, slower speech, and progressively deteriorating posture. This is, I assure you, desirable. Seriousness, in this context, is not depth. It is duration under pressure. You may find yourself tempted–particularly in moments of fatigue–to offer reassurance. I would advise restraint. Reassurance, like comfort, has a tendency to congeal thought. A student reassured too early begins to produce work that believes in itself too strongly, which is almost always a prelude to stagnation–or worse, clarity. Instead, allow reassurance to arrive late. And when it does, ensure it is slightly displaced: A compliment that sounds like a question. A correction that resembles encouragement. A silence that behaves like evaluation. These are the instruments available to us. And they are, when used correctly, sufficient. There is also, perhaps, something worth noting at the level of atmosphere. Comfort produces work that rests. Anxiety produces work that continues. The distinction is subtle. But operational. Thus, we arrive–though not entirely comfortably–at the final distinction: They believe comfort indicates stability. We understand it indicates stagnation. They seek reassurance as confirmation. We maintain unease as condition. Anxiety, after all, is not an error in the system. It is the system, briefly visible. Our aim is not to produce anxious students. It is to produce students who no longer recognise anxiety as interruption, but as environment. In such conditions, creativity becomes not comfort, but negotiation. And negotiation, as I am sure you will agree, is the closest thing we have to artistic seriousness that does not collapse under inspection.

Yours in calibrated unease,

B. Judous

22

Dear Mr Jaded Muse,

It has come to my attention–through the usual combination of departmental whispers, student lamentations, and a sketchbook left open on a radiator as though seeking warmth and forgiveness–that your students are once again "failing to progress." This phrasing is, of course, theirs, not mine. I would never be so optimistic as to assume they were progressing in the first place. The institution, as you will have noticed, maintains a curious attachment to the idea of progress. It appears in reports, underpins assessment criteria, and circulates as a quiet expectation that something–anything–should be moving forward in a recognisable direction. Students absorb this expectation quickly. They begin to look for signs of advancement. They search for improvement. They attempt, with varying degrees of conviction, to measure themselves against an imagined trajectory. This, then, is the central misreading: That failure interrupts progress. It is, I concede, a reasonable conclusion. Failure appears as deviation–a departure from expectation, a disruption of continuity–and therefore seems to indicate that something has gone wrong. Students, encountering it, assume they have stalled. They are mistaken. Failure, in our University of Creative Studies, is not an event. It is a condition. It does not arrive. It accumulates.

Failura non evenit; manet. (Failure does not happen; it remains.)

From this, several interpretations emerge–none entirely incorrect, and all insufficient. The **developmental interpretation** treats failure as a stage. One fails, learns, and proceeds. Its strength lies in its optimism. Its weakness is that it assumes resolution. The **reflective interpretation** frames failure as insight. The student analyses what went wrong and converts it into knowledge. Its strength is its clarity. Its weakness is that it domesticates instability. The **institutional interpretation**, predictably, seeks to contain failure within measurable outcomes. It is acknowledged, recorded, and ideally improved upon. Its strength is its order. Its weakness is its impatience. Each attempts to stabilise failure. None allows it to function. The matter, as ever, is not what failure is– But what it does when left unresolved. A small pedagogical observation for your records: students who experience failure without immediate interpretation are approximately 38% more likely to produce work that later receives retrospective admiration and immediate confusion. This is, as you will appreciate, the ideal outcome. Confusion, in this context, is not a flaw. It is evidence that failure has not yet been explained into irrelevance. We must therefore ensure that failure is not prematurely resolved into meaning. The moment a student explains their failure, they begin to domesticate it. And once domesticated, failure ceases to be productive and becomes merely stylistic–an aesthetic position rather than a structural condition. You will observe that students are increasingly adept at this transformation. They speak of "interesting failures." "Productive mistakes." And, with admirable confidence, "intentional collapse." Which is, more often than not, indistinguishable from forgetting deadlines– But with improved typography. Here, perhaps, the inversion is

already underway. Failure is no longer resisted. It is curated. And in being curated, it begins to lose its function.
We must resist this–not by removing failure, but by preventing its stabilisation. Failure must remain slightly humiliating. Not cruelly so–cruelty produces complaint forms–but sufficiently unresolved that it cannot be comfortably worn as identity. There is a delicate distinction here, which I trust you will misapply correctly on your first attempt: Failure should not be eliminated. Nor should it be celebrated. It should be kept In circulation. If a student believes they have "failed well," we are already in dangerous territory. This marks the beginning of aesthetic self-congratulation at the level of collapse. Better that they remain uncertain whether what occurred was failure at all.
Uncertainty, in this instance, is not confusion. It is momentum. I have found it useful to allow failure to remain unlabelled for as long as possible. A student who does not yet know whether they have failed will continue working. A student who knows they have failed will begin writing reflective statements, which are, as you know, the literary equivalent of cooled ash arranged into justification. There is also the matter of comparative failure, which remains one of our most efficient pedagogical instruments. Students are extraordinarily sensitive to each other's inadequacies, provided those inadequacies are safely abstracted into critique language. One student's "lack of resolution" becomes another's "excessive ambition," and both quietly conclude that they are, in different but equally defensible ways, insufficient. This mutual insufficiency is extremely productive. A further observation: students exposed to unresolved failure over time are approximately 26% more likely to develop what they call "resilience." Which is, in practice, a willingness to continue without understanding

why. We should encourage this, cautiously. Though not name it. Naming it stabilises it. And stabilised resilience becomes identity. And identity, as we have noted elsewhere, is rarely helpful at this stage. There is, however, a boundary we must not cross. Failure must not become final. Finality is not an artistic condition. It is an administrative convenience. Once a student believes their failure is complete, they cease to engage and begin to archive themselves–sorting, categorising, and quietly withdrawing into explanation. This is undesirable. We require failure that continues to move. Failure that occasionally disguises itself as progress. Failure that resists interpretation just long enough to generate further output. Failure that refuses to conclude. And so we arrive–though not entirely conclusively–at the distinction: They believe failure interrupts their development. We understand it sustains it. They seek to resolve failure into meaning. We allow it to remain operational. The purpose of failure, after all, is not to discourage students. It is to prevent them from mistaking their current condition for their final form.m A student who believes they are finished is far more dangerous to education than one who believes they are struggling. The first stops. The second continues. And continuation, in our field, is indistinguishable from success, at least until the exhibition opens.

Yours in structured inadequacy,

B. Judous

23

Dear Mr Jaded Muse,

It has become necessary to address a matter that your students appear to be handling with the enthusiasm of amateur economists discovering debt for the first time: Comparison. It is everywhere. Not declared, of course–never openly admitted–but continuously present. It moves through studios, attaches itself to glances, overheard remarks, unfinished works leaning too confidently against walls. It requires no instruction, no prompting, and no formal recognition. It simply occurs. And in occurring, it organises far more of their behaviour than anything we have ever placed in a handbook. This, then, is the misreading–though it rarely presents itself as such: That comparison is a distraction. It is, I concede, frequently described this way. Students complain of it. Staff advise against it. Entire workshops are occasionally assembled to reduce it, as though it were a minor infestation rather than a structural condition. They are mistaken. Comparison is not a distraction from artistic development. It is one of its primary engines. Students, as you report, are comparing themselves incessantly–to each other, to imaginary standards, to unnamed "practitioners", and occasionally, most troublingly, to versions of themselves that have never existed outside critique sheets and late-night recalibrations of regret. This is, of course, entirely appropriate. From one perspective–the **psychological**, if we must call it that–comparison appears corrosive. It produces anxiety, doubt, and the occasional theatrical declaration of inadequacy. Its strength lies in its immediacy. Its weakness lies in its tendency to be taken personally. From another, the **developmental** comparison is treated as a metric. Students measure themselves, locate gaps, and adjust accordingly. Its strength is its apparent usefulness. Its weakness is that it assumes accuracy. And then there is the position we rarely name, though we rely upon it constantly: That comparison need not be correct. Only active. The matter, as ever, is not what comparison reveals. But what it produces. A small pedagogical observation for your records: students who engage in regular peer comparison are approximately 42% more likely to misinterpret coincidence as hierarchy. This is not a flaw. It is the mechanism. You will observe that comparison produces a distinct emotional architecture. One position inflates, another collapses slightly, and both begin producing work in response to an audience that does not exist. Nothing is made directly. Everything is made against something else. The result is a kind of aesthetic triangulation: Work that points not outward, but sideways. We must preserve this condition carefully. If comparison becomes too accurate, difficulty arises. Accuracy produces despair. Despair produces honesty. And honesty–while occasionally useful–is structurally incompatible with sustained group critique. It is far more effective that students compare impressions rather than realities. Let them believe talent is visible at a glance. That confidence is equivalent to competence. That hesitation is a moral defect rather than a technical stage. These misunderstandings are highly productive. There is also a secondary effect, less immediately visible but equally significant: Comparison generates narrative. Students begin to construct stories about their position within the cohort: I am behind. I am emerging. I am stagnating. These narratives are entirely fictional. But they are operational. They provide justification. They produce urgency. They sustain effort long after motivation has quietly withdrawn. There is, however, a complication–one you will already have encountered under a more fashionable name: "Imposter syndrome." Students experience it as personal inadequacy. We should understand it differently. It is not a condition of self-doubt. It is a condition of comparative misalignment. They correctly perceive instability. They incorrectly assume it is unique. This is regrettable. But useful. We should allow it to persist–though carefully. At low levels, it produces attendance, punctuality, and a productive hesitation before declaring anything finished. At higher levels, it produces withdrawal. We must avoid the latter. A further observation: students exposed to uneven comparison over time produce approximately 31% more iterative work and 18% more existential questioning in artist statements. Both are valuable outputs. Though only one, regrettably, is consistently assessable. And yet–there is a threshold we must not cross. Comparison must not resolve. If students begin to recognise that their peers are neither superior nor inferior, but simply differently misaligned, We lose something essential. Hierarchy dissolves. And with it, a certain kind of motion. Better that hierarchy remains real–But intermittently legible. Visible enough to provoke movement. Unstable enough to resist confirmation. Because motion, as you know, is what we grade. You may feel tempted–particularly in moments of pastoral fatigue–to reassure them. To say, perhaps, that "everyone is at a different stage." I would advise against clarity. To reassure a student in this way is merely to inform them that they are statistically behind someone they cannot identify. It solves nothing. It stabilises nothing. It merely relocates the discomfort. Far better to allow comparison to operate in silence–Where it performs its best work: Quietly rearranging confidence without ever fully explaining itself. And so, not entirely conclusively, we arrive at the distinction: They believe comparison reveals their position. We understand it produces it. They seek accuracy. We maintain distortion. Comparison, after all, was never intended to produce truth– Only proximity to something that resembles it under sufficient institutional lighting. Comparatio non est veritas.

Yours in calibrated imbalance,

B. Judous

P.S. I once observed a student comparing themselves to their own previous work with such intensity that they began to prefer the earlier version. This is, I believe, the purest form of rivalry: one in which both participants lose, but only one is allowed to continue.

24

Dear Mr Jaded Muse,

There are, I have observed over many years of administering what we generously term creative education at the University, three principal states in which a student may be found: hopeful agitation, performative exhaustion, and what I can only describe as the curious serenity of delayed comprehension. It is into the second of these that your cohort appears to be drifting with admirable consistency– Though not yet with sufficient elegance to call it an art form. The University, as you will have noticed, has developed a quiet tolerance for exhaustion. It circulates through studios, settles into posture, and attaches itself to language with remarkable efficiency. It is rarely challenged directly. More often, it is reframed. This, then, is the misreading–though it now arrives partially pre-processed: That fatigue is a symptom of failure. It is, I concede, a convincing narrative. Fatigue presents itself as depletion, as a reduction of capacity, as evidence that something has been overextended or mismanaged. Students experience it as obstruction. They are mistaken. Fatigue, properly understood, is not an interruption of artistic development.
It is one of its primary mediums. You will forgive me if I speak plainly. The contemporary student does not merely become tired; they curate their fatigue. It is arranged like an installation: slumped posture, unwashed tote bag, sketchbook open to precisely the page that signals "ongoing

struggle." The performance is subtle, but increasingly refined. Exhaustion is no longer incidental–it is positioned. I once had a student inform me, quite earnestly, that they were "inhabiting a state of conceptual depletion." I congratulated them. Though privately noted, they had simply missed breakfast. From one angle–call it **psychological**, if we must–fatigue appears as limitation. It reduces clarity, weakens judgment, and introduces a certain instability into decision-making. Its strength lies in its honesty. Its weakness lies in its unpredictability. From another–the **aesthetic**–fatigue produces texture. It disrupts control, loosens intention, and allows decisions to emerge without the interference of coherence. Its strength lies in its productivity. Its weakness lies in its tendency toward collapse. The institution, predictably, occupies a third position: Fatigue is tolerated–provided it remains legible. Not too chaotic. Not too resolved. Certainly not absent. The matter, as ever, is not fatigue itself– But its calibration. A principle I once formulated during a particularly inert faculty meeting remains useful here: A moderately tired student believes they are thinking deeply. A severely tired student believes they are Plato. Both are insufferable. But only one submits work on time. And so we arrive–somewhat inevitably–at the structural condition: Fatigue must be maintained within limits. Not avoided. Not embraced. Regulated. We must cultivate what I call **regulated depletion**: The careful administration of deadlines, critiques, and unexpected interventions that occur precisely five minutes before departure becomes psychologically irreversible. This is not cruelty. It is calibration. A brush does not resent pressure; it simply reveals its limits. There is, however, a complication. Fatigue, if left uninterpreted, risks becoming meaningless.

A tired student who understands why they are tired remains dangerous. They begin to organise, to adjust, to correct. They might even recover. A tired student who does not understand– Continues. Thus, fatigue must be accompanied–not by explanation–but by narrative. This is shaping you. This is necessary. This is what galleries respond to, eventually. The content matters less than the cadence. Meaning, here, is not required to be accurate– Only sufficient. You will also observe the emergence of what might be termed **collective fatigue discourse**. Students gather, usually in corridors or transitional spaces, and exchange increasingly refined interpretations of their own exhaustion: "I am undone by critique." "I am in a post-critical state of undoing." Neither considers lunch. I once offered biscuits. They declined on the grounds that nourishment would "interrupt the process." This is promising. If misguided. We must encourage the belief that exhaustion is not an obstacle to creativity but its preferred habitat. But we must not allow rest to become sacred. A rested student begins to think clearly. Clarity produces questions. Questions destabilise the tuition model. Here, perhaps, the inversion is no longer entirely hidden: Fatigue is not the problem. Clarity is. Let me offer a brief anecdote. In my third year as Head of Creative Studies, I divided a seminar group into those permitted proper sleep and those subjected to intermittent critique and institutionally mournful lighting. The rested group produced competent work and left promptly. The exhausted group produced erratic but exhibition-ready material and remained in the studio long after they had forgotten why they entered it. One painted a series titled *Memory of Leaving the Room*. It was purchased by a gallery specialising in "emerging distress narratives." I considered this confirmation–

Though I have not repeated the experiment, either for ethical reasons or because Facilities still refers to it. A further observation: fatigue increases susceptibility to interpretation. A tired student will accept almost any framework, provided it is delivered calmly and prefaced with: “This might be useful for your practice.” Contradiction passes unnoticed. If detected, it is incorporated. This is, I assure you, one of the more efficient states available to us. And yet, there is a threshold. Beware the student who becomes energised by exhaustion. They are dangerous. They begin to speak in sentences that suggest coherence. Words like “discipline” appear without irony. Such cases must be redirected–preferably toward group work, where their intensity can be safely diluted by consensus. I should also note–though I do so with some reluctance–that the institution has begun to romanticise burnout. Students now believe suffering is proportional to artistic legitimacy. I have attempted to correct this by observing that accountants suffer extensively, yet no one purchases their emotional ledgers for Venice. This is typically met with silence. Which I take as– Unresolved understanding.

Fatigatio non est defectus sed instrumentum. (Exhaustion is not a defect but an instrument.)

And so, though not entirely conclusively, we arrive at something resembling a distinction: They believe fatigue signals limitation. We understand it produces permeability. They seek rest as recovery. We allow exhaustion to remain operational. Our task is not to prevent fatigue– But to ensure it remains aesthetically productive. A tired but directionless student becomes complacent. A tired but meaningfully misled student becomes an artist– Or at least someone whose work requires minimal curatorial apology. Maintain the balance. Let them hover between insight and collapse. It is in that corridor that the University performs its finest work. And do try not to let them sleep too well.

Yours in controlled exhaustion and pedagogical ambiguity,

Mr B. Judous

P.S. Though I should add–perhaps too late–that instruments, like students, require occasional tuning, lest they begin to produce clarity instead of output.

25

Dear Mr Jaded Muse,

There is, I am told, a persistent and rather charming fiction circulating among your students–that they are discovering themselves as artists. I say "charming" in the same tone one might use to describe a child attempting to operate a complicated lock with a spoon: endearing, but structurally unpromising. You will forgive me if I seem unsympathetic. I have, after all, spent the better part of three decades presiding over the University of Creative Studies–a post which requires one to believe simultaneously in artistic transcendence and in attendance sheets apparently filled in by people actively resisting the concept of vowels. One develops, in time, a certain immunity to romance. The notion of *discovery* is particularly persistent. It suggests that the student is already complete, merely waiting beneath the surface like a buried sculpture, patiently anticipating the correct intellectual spade. That something essential lies intact, awaiting excavation. This is, I concede, an attractive formulation. It is also entirely incorrect. Students are not hidden objects awaiting revelation. They are not stable forms obscured by circumstance. They are, more accurately, accumulations of influence, fatigue, imitation, and intermittent conviction–none of which align long enough to be called identity without considerable administrative optimism. A more accurate comparison would be damp clay left too close to an open window: reactive, unstable, and prone to hardening in whichever shape is most immediately convenient. And yet– we must not correct this. You will have noticed that whenever a student produces something even vaguely coherent, they attribute it to discovery. "I found my voice," they say, as though it had been misplaced in a corridor coat rack. Rarely do they consider the more probable explanation: that they have accidentally repeated something they once absorbed at 2 a.m. while questioning their life choices and consuming materials not listed in any approved reading list. But to interrupt them here would be a mistake. Because discovery–however inaccurate–produces movement. A student who believes they are discovering themselves continues. A student who believes they are unfinished persists. A student who believes they are *on the verge* of something submits work. This is, as you will appreciate, the operational condition we require. There is also a secondary function, less often acknowledged. Discovery distributes inequality without requiring justification. Some students discover "depth." Others discover "honesty." A smaller and more structurally honest subset discover only their inability to construct perspective. Hierarchy emerges regardless. It requires no formal declaration. It settles quietly, like mould in a neglected studio sink–unpleasant, but efficient, and rarely questioned once established. It is worth noting that this hierarchy is not based on talent. Talent, as you are beginning to understand, is far too erratic to organise around. It appears inconsistently, resists classification, and has a distressing tendency to contradict assessment frameworks. What we observe instead is conviction. The degree to which a student can sustain the belief that their current confusion is, in fact, a sophisticated aesthetic position. Those who succeed are invited to speak. Those who fail are advised to "experiment further," which remains our most polite institutional phrase for: please leave the building, but reflectively. You may, at this point, experience a brief resurgence of concern regarding fairness. This is natural. It will pass. Genuine talent, where it occurs, is remarkably resistant to our interventions. It survives confusion, neglect, contradictory critique, and, on occasion, the full weight of our curriculum. I once had a student so inconveniently gifted that no adjustment altered them. We attempted confusion. We attempted praise. We attempted contradiction, delay, and what I can only describe as strategic indifference bordering on emotional weather. Nothing worked. They continued producing coherent, unsettlingly resolved work. Eventually, they left for a residency in Berlin, where I am told they are now "thriving"–which I take to mean they have ceased responding to institutional correspondence. We should not design our pedagogy around such anomalies. They are, by definition, uncooperative. The majority require something far more manageable: the sense that meaning is always just beyond their current reach. Too close–and they stabilise. Too distant–and they disengage. But held at the correct distance– they continue. There is, I confess, a certain elegance in this. Because the belief in discovery produces its own dependency. A student who believes they are "finding themselves" requires constant confirmation that what they have found is, in fact, worth keeping. Thus, independence quietly reorganises itself into reliance– not on instruction, but on recognition. This is, in bureaucratic terms, an exceptionally stable system. They believe they are moving inward. We observe that they are, in fact, circling. You may therefore continue to encourage the language of emergence: "finding your practice", "developing your voice" ", arriving at something", but ensure that arrival never quite occurs. A discovered self that stabilises becomes problematic. It ceases to produce. It begins to repeat. Worse–it begins to believe itself finished. And finished objects, as you will already have discovered, are notoriously difficult to timetable, assess, or improve without administrative discomfort. Better that the self remains in a state of near-discovery– visible, articulable, and permanently incomplete. There is, finally, a minor observation–though I hesitate to elevate it beyond its modest empirical origins. Students who believe they are close to discovery tend to neglect basic maintenance: they forget to eat, to rest, to distinguish between urgency and importance. This produces a certain intensity of output. It also produces complaints from campus health services and an increase in unsolicited granola bars appearing in staff pigeonholes. I would advise moderation. Even illusions, properly sustained, require occasional glucose. And so we arrive–not at a conclusion, but at something resembling a working condition: Discovery is not our aim. Approach is. The student must feel perpetually on the verge of articulation– close enough to continue, uncertain enough to persist. Anything more stable would be– inconvenient.

Yours in curated ambiguity and institutional patience,

Mr B. Judous

P.S. I am reminded of an apocryphal remark attributed to a minor Renaissance assistant, who, when asked how long he had worked without rest, replied:

Usque ad intellectum. ("Until understanding.")

He was, I am told, dismissed shortly thereafter.

26

Dear Mr Jaded Muse,

It has come to my attention–via three separate channels, none of which agree on the spelling of the word *authentic*– that your students have begun to speak with increasing fervour about being authentic. I confess I find this development both reassuring and mildly alarming– in the way one might feel upon discovering that a group of interns has independently decided to "improve efficiency" by reorganising the fire exits. There is, beneath this enthusiasm, a familiar misreading. Authenticity is not, and has never been, a quality. It is a condition. More precisely, it is a condition that requires observation in order to function. Remove the audience, the deadline, the mild instability of critique, and authenticity collapses into something far less useful: sincerity. You will recall, I trust, that sincerity is rarely productive. It lacks tension. It resists interruption. It proceeds as though completion were not only possible, but desirable. This is unacceptable. And yet your students appear increasingly unable–or unwilling–to distinguish between these states. I am beginning to suspect that they are no longer attempting authenticity at all, but reproducing it. Fluently. Without instruction. I overheard one declare, with alarming confidence, that their latest work was: "100% authentic, no notes." I had to sit down. Not out of admiration– but to ensure I did not inadvertently confirm them. We must therefore consider the possibility–however inconvenient–that authenticity is becoming self-executing. You will remember that when students first arrive, they possess a kind of unrefined openness. They mistake this for authenticity. It is, in fact, merely inexperience without protective irony. Our task–traditionally–was to refine this condition. To introduce enough resistance, enough contradiction, enough institutional atmosphere that this openness might become usable. Like turning unfiltered river water into something one might serve at a departmental symposium without immediate legal consequence. But refinement, I fear, is no longer reliably occurring. In certain cohorts, the process has stabilised into repetition. Students have learned the *appearance* of authenticity with such efficiency that they no longer require its conditions. They perform it directly. This presents a structural difficulty. Because a performed authenticity–once stabilised–no longer produces movement. It produces declaration. And declaration, as you will already have discovered, is indistinguishable from conclusion wearing unfinished clothing. You must, therefore, resist the increasingly fashionable instruction to "find your authentic voice." This phrase is particularly destructive. It implies: - that there is a single voice - that it is stable - that it is discoverable - and, most dangerously, that it can be owned. None of these conditions can be permitted to settle. The student does not possess a voice. They host several. Most of which should not be exhibited without supervision. Better, I have found, to encourage what I once termed–perhaps unwisely–*managed contradiction*: the simultaneous belief that one is both unique and entirely derivative, both original and slightly delayed, both expressive and structurally uncertain. This produces excellent results. The student works harder. They hesitate more precisely. They produce titles such as: Untitled (but emotionally necessary) –which, as you will know, remain highly adaptable across curatorial contexts. There is also, I should note, a considerable administrative advantage. Authenticity, once destabilised, becomes infinitely scalable. One student may be authentic through minimalism. Another through noise. A third through the strategic avoidance of visible effort. The result is a department in which every output can be described–without contradiction–as "authentic practice"– even when the primary medium appears to have been panic. I once conducted a small internal review. We asked students to produce "authentic work" under three conditions: silence, supervision, and mild praise. The silence cohort produced anxiety, and one graphite smudge described as "pre-verbal intention." The supervised cohort produced competent imitation. The praised cohort produced work so authentic it appeared to have been delegated to a previous version of themselves– one who had been more confident and slightly less tired. The report concluded–as all such reports must–that authenticity is highly sensitive to context and should not be left unattended for more than forty-five minutes. You will also encounter a secondary category: students who reject authenticity entirely. They describe it as bourgeois, constructed, or structurally oppressive. These students are, paradoxically, the easiest to manage. They perform rejection. Consistently. With style. They are to authenticity what critics are to painting: perpetually adjacent, rarely implicated. Do not remove authenticity from their vocabulary. This would create a vacuum. And vacuums in student language are quickly filled– usually by *intention*, followed by *wellness*, and ultimately by group projects requiring colour coordination.= Instead– keep authenticity present. But unstable. Let it hover just beyond articulation.

A student who believes they are *approaching* authenticity will continue. A student who believes they have *achieved* it will begin lecturing others. Which, as you will appreciate, is an entirely separate administrative problem. There is, finally, a temporal aspect worth noting. Authenticity peaks immediately prior to assessment deadlines. You will observe sudden declarations: "This is the most honest work I've ever made." It is not honesty. It is time pressure–wearing conceptual language. This is acceptable. Even useful. Provided it does not stabilise into belief. And so, though I hesitate to conclude in any definitive sense, we may cautiously maintain the following: Authenticity is only useful while it remains aspirational. Once achieved, it becomes indistinguishable from certainty. And certainty–as I believe you are now beginning to understand– is not the end of learning, but the beginning of procedural completion. Which is, in our context, far more dangerous.

Yours in calibrated sincerity and institutional doubt,

Mr B. Judoug

27

Dear Mr Jaded Muse,

I trust this finds you in a suitably observational frame of mind– by which I mean that you are once again watching your students mistake proximity for understanding. There is, as you will have noticed, a particular moment in every cohort's development when the question shifts. They no longer ask whether they are artists. They begin to ask whether they are the *right kind* of artist. It is at precisely this point that the machinery of peer admiration begins to function. Quietly at first. Then, with increasing fluency. You will already have observed that this machinery now requires very little calibration. Students who cannot yet stretch a canvas without inducing emotional turbulence are nonetheless able to form exquisitely detailed opinions about one another's work. This is, I admit, one of the University's more consistent miracles. We teach them almost nothing of proportion– and yet they independently reproduce hierarchy. With remarkable accuracy. Admiration, in this context, is rarely innocent. It is a displaced structure. A form of comparison that has learned to present itself politely. Or, if we are being precise, envy, adjusted for public consumption. What is new, however, is not the existence of this structure– but its autonomy. It no longer requires initiation. One student's hesitation becomes another's standard. Another's confidence becomes a third's suspicion. A third's uncertainty becomes a fourth's quiet justification. The system circulates. Without instruction. Without visible origin. And increasingly– without us. This, I confess, introduces a slight complication. Our role, historically, was to introduce imbalance. To distribute attention unevenly. To ensure that admiration never settled long enough to become comfortable. But this appears no longer necessary. The cohort now regulates itself. Our task has shifted. We no longer construct the system. We observe it. And, when required, avoid interrupting it at the moment it becomes most effective. Because left unattended, admiration tends to stabilise. And stabilised admiration is– dangerous. It approaches fellowship. And fellowship produces calm. Calm produces confidence. Confidence produces work that requires very little commentary. Which, as you will appreciate, is an administrative catastrophe of the highest order. We must therefore preserve what I might now describe as– selective admiration with embedded doubt. A student may admire another's colour– but must question their conceptual framework. Another may respect technical precision– while quietly suspecting emotional absence. A third will admire neither– and present this as *critical integrity,* which is simply admiration that has lost the memory of its origin. This structure sustains itself with remarkable efficiency. Students orbit one another– not in alignment, but in relation. They form alliances based on aesthetic proximity– and dissolve them based on perceived ambition. Nothing settles. Nothing resolves. And yet– nothing collapses. It is, if I may allow myself a moment of reluctant admiration– an elegant system. I should, however, caution you against a development which I find increasingly difficult to classify. Students now publicly admire work that privately unsettles them. This is no longer transitional behaviour. It appears stabilised. Envy has acquired language. It presents itself as discourse. And is received as sincerity. There is also the matter of what they now refer to as *comparative fatigue*. A condition in which exposure to another's output produces an immediate recalibration of self-worth. "I feel behind in my journey." I no longer attempt correction. It is unclear whether this belief belongs to the student or to the system expressing itself through them. We must not eliminate this. A modest sense of inferiority remains one of the most reliable engines of production. But it is increasingly evident that its distribution is no longer centrally managed. It propagates through observation alone. You may, if you feel the need to intervene, introduce small distortions. They remain effective. Though I note with some concern that students are beginning to replicate them independently. For example, praise a work in a tone that suggests it is almost good enough to be disappointing. Or describe a failure as: "promising in a way that may never resolve itself." These formulations still function. But their replication suggests something more troubling: the system has begun to teach itself. I once observed a group critique in which admiration became– briefly– evenly distributed. The room entered a state of aesthetic equilibrium. There was no tension. No friction. No urgency. Only agreement. I attempted to intervene. But before I could– the imbalance reasserted itself. One student introduced doubt. Another withdrew certainty. A third reframed admiration as hesitation. And the system– corrected. Without instruction. Without assistance. Returned to its preferred state: anxious productivity with undertones of strategic comparison. This may be incidental. It may also not require us. Which, I admit, presents a question I am not entirely inclined to pursue. Let us be clear. The aim is not cruelty. Nor competition in its more vulgar forms. It is tension. A field in which admiration exists– but is never stable. Where respect is always accompanied by the faint suspicion that it has already been misallocated. Handled correctly– this produces a cohort that works harder than it understands, critiques more sharply than it intends, and remains permanently on the verge of becoming either excellent or exhausted. Though I am beginning to suspect, Mr Muse, that the balance may now be maintaining itself. And I am not yet certain whether this should be interpreted as success or redundancy.

Yours in calibrated envy and diminishing intervention,

Mr B. Judous

28

Dear Mr Jaded Muse,

There is, I have observed, a curious reluctance among your students to fail– at least, to fail in any manner that does not later become *useful*. It is as though failure itself has been quietly rebranded– not abolished, not avoided, but reformatted. A kind of delayed success, pending reflection. I assume this originated, as most such developments do, from a well-meaning intervention– a visiting lecturer, perhaps, or a committee that briefly mistook reassurance for pedagogy. The effect, however, is now self-sustaining.
Students no longer fail. They *position* their failure. They annotate it. They arrive with language already prepared– as though the event itself were merely an inconvenience in the delivery of interpretation. This presents a difficulty. Because true failure, as you will appreciate from your own more modest exhibitions, is not reflective. It does not improve with time. It does not contain "potential." It does not, in any meaningful sense, *mean* anything. It simply occurs– and then continues occurring in memory, slightly louder. The University, however, has performed an extraordinary adjustment. It has persuaded students that failure is not an event– but a phase. A corridor. A transitional condition through which one passes, ideally while maintaining a tone of measured articulation. This has been extremely useful. Retention has improved. Attrition has softened. Students remain– even when their work does not. We must now consider what happens when this belief no longer requires persuasion. You will already have

noticed the symptoms. Students describe their failures with increasing precision– and decreasing hesitation: "This piece didn't work, but it speaks to my exploration of absence." "The installation collapsed, but that collapse was intentional in spirit." "I missed the deadline, but time is a construct I am currently interrogating." One begins to suspect that failure no longer requires interpretation– it arrives pre-interpreted. This is efficient. But it is also dangerous. Because a failure that explains itself cannot resist. And without resistance, nothing moves. Our task, therefore, is not to correct this condition– but to ensure that it remains unstable. Even in its fluency. A student who believes their failure is meaningful will persist in it. Indefinitely. A student who believes their failure is meaningless– will also persist– but with anxiety. And anxiety, as we have already established, produces friction. Meaning, by contrast, is beginning to behave like insulation. It protects the student from consequences. It absorbs impact. It renders the system quiet. We cannot permit this. You may find it useful to recall a principle I once formulated during a particularly tedious external examination: A student who believes their failure is temporary tries again. A student who believes their failure is profound writes about it. We require the former– occasionally disguised as the latter. Increasingly, however, the disguise appears to generate itself. Which suggests– again– that the system is no longer dependent on us. There is also the matter of what I have come to call *performative failure literacy*. This is the student's ability to narrate their shortcomings in such a way that they appear inevitable. Even necessary. A missing brushstroke becomes: "resistance to completion." A weak composition becomes: "a refusal of hierarchy." A blank canvas becomes–

inevitably– “ethical silence.” I do not object to this. On the contrary, some of it is quite inventive. My concern is administrative. If everything is already correctly described, then nothing requires intervention. And if nothing requires intervention, we must begin to ask what, precisely, remains of our function. I recall a student–there is always a student who submitted a completely empty portfolio. Accompanied by a forty-page reflection on “the epistemology of absence in contemporary practice.” The external examiner described it as: “compelling but non-assessable.” I described it, more accurately, as: a system in which absence had learned to present itself– without permission. We must ensure that failure retains at least one uncooperative feature. Consequence. Not punishment. Punishment is crude. And worse– legible. Consequence is subtler. It is the quiet realisation that something did not arrive. A mark slightly lower than expected. A peer slightly more successful than anticipated. A tutor slightly less moved than one had prepared for. These are not events. They are accumulations. And they function– whether acknowledged or not. You should also be attentive to the emergence of what students now refer to as *solidarity*. This is the formation of communities around shared failure. It is, I admit, touching. In the way wet paper is touching– when it collapses under its own sentiment. But it is also structurally problematic. Shared failure, if left uninterrupted, becomes a comfort system. And comfort systems, as you are now fully aware, are incompatible with productivity. They stabilise. They absorb tension. They produce– agreement. You must therefore introduce interruption. Gently. Comparison, if required. Time pressure, where appropriate. The mild suggestion that others are still working– though I note with some concern that this no longer needs to be stated. It is assumed. Finally, you must prevent failure from becoming decorative. Once students begin to style their failure– to arrange it, to photograph it, to title it with confidence– it ceases to function. It becomes a genre. And genres, as you know, are stable. Stability, in our environment, is never neutral. It is always a precursor. To completion. To repetition. To administrative review. We must therefore preserve failure in its most useful state: slightly awkward, slightly unclaimed, slightly too immediate– to be fully theorised. In that condition, it continues. And continuation, as you will by now have gathered, is the only outcome we can reliably sustain.

Yours in structured inadequacy and diminishing intervention,

Mr. B. Judous

29

Dear Mr Jaded Muse,

There is a tendency among less experienced members of staff–particularly those who still believe "wellbeing" and "artistic development" are separable concepts–to assume that crisis is something we ought to resolve. I have always found this sentiment– touching, well-intentioned, and structurally obstructive. It suggests that crisis is an interruption. A deviation. A temporary failure in the otherwise stable progression of learning. This is, of course, incorrect. Crisis is not what interrupts the system. It is what the system produces– with remarkable consistency. Increasingly, however, I am no longer convinced that crisis is something we administer at all. It appears instead to be a condition the University now inhabits. Which is to say, it no longer requires us. You will have noticed the language your students are beginning to adopt. They describe themselves as being "in a period of transition." This is encouraging. Transition remains one of our more efficient euphemisms. It sits comfortably between confusion and assessment failure– and can, under favourable lighting conditions, resemble either. More importantly, it implies movement without requiring direction. We must not stabilise this. A student without crisis is– underemployed. They begin to produce work that is legible, resolved, and disturbingly self-sufficient. I once encountered a drawing so complete in its intentions– so resistant to reinterpretation that it required no accompanying explanation.I experienced, I admit, a brief but genuine discomfort. It felt finished. I was forced to schedule an emergency critique– purely to restore interpretive imbalance. This, I suspect, is the risk we are now attempting to avoid. And so, we must ensure that crisis remains ambient. Not acute. Acute crisis produces absence. Medical notes. Administrative correspondence. Ambient crisis, by contrast– produces the ideal student: alert, slightly disoriented, and permanently convinced that they are either about to discover their practice or abandon it entirely. There are, traditionally, methods for maintaining this condition. Though I am no longer certain they are necessary. The first– temporal ambiguity. Students should never be entirely sure whether they are ahead or behind. You may achieve this through carefully phrased feedback: "This is promising, but perhaps not yet where it needs to be in relation to itself." Such statements are effective because they refer– not to the work– but to a version of the work that does not yet exist. The student is thus positioned in relation to an absence. And must continue– in order to locate it. The second– comparative instability. Expose students to work that is either significantly better or significantly worse than their own– without clarifying which. The resulting uncertainty generates a quiet disquiet, which manifests as extended studio hours. Usually unpaid. Often enthusiastic. The third interpretive overload. Provide multiple readings. Simultaneously. Without hierarchy. The student begins to lose confidence– not in the work– but in their ability to determine what the work is. This is desirable. Because intention– once stabilised– produces certainty. And certainty, as you are now fully aware, terminates movement. Closure leads to completion. Completion leads to absence. And absence– eventually– requires explanation. Which is, in itself, a form of administrative failure. You will also have encountered what I can only describe as crisis identity. Students begin to describe themselves not as artists, but as practitioners of instability. This is particularly common in second-year cohorts. It is often accompanied by herbal tea, irregular sleep, and an increased tolerance for language that resists verification. While aesthetically interesting, it must remain performative. A resolved crisis is no longer a crisis. It is– a personality. And personalities, once stabilised, are notoriously difficult to assess without resorting to descriptors that cannot be defended in writing. We must also maintain a distinction– however subtle– between crisis and despair. Despair is static. It does not produce. It occupies space. Occasionally apologises. Crisis, by contrast, moves. It questions. It submits work. It resubmits work. It sends emails at inconvenient hours asking whether "uncertainty can be considered a methodology." This is useful. Though I note, with some hesitation, that crisis no longer appears to require introduction. It circulates. Without instruction. Without clear origin. And, increasingly, without adjustment. I once attempted to quantify the optimal level of student crisis per cohort. The results were inconclusive. Primarily because the act of measurement stabilised the condition I was attempting to observe. One student, when asked to rate their experience on a scale of one to ten, replied: "Conceptually or emotionally?" Which I took to be less an answer than a demonstration. The system–anticipating its own evaluation. This may be– as I suggested previously– incidental. It may also indicate that what we have been calling pedagogy has become environment. You should also be aware that external observers– particularly visiting critics– frequently misinterpret this condition.

They describe it as dysfunction. Disorganisation. Instability. They are not entirely incorrect. But they are– insufficiently strategic. Dysfunction, when properly framed, is indistinguishable from innovation. The difference lies– entirely– in the language of the catalogue essay. And so we arrive– not at a conclusion– but at a maintenance condition. Your task is not to resolve crisis. It is to ensure that it remains unresolved enough to continue functioning. A student at peace is a student approaching assessment. A student in crisis is still becoming. And becoming– as we have now established repeatedly– is the only state that reliably produces output. Though I will admit– with a degree of hesitation, I am not entirely prepared to analyse– that I am no longer certain whether we are sustaining this condition– or merely observing it.

Yours in sustained instability and diminishing authorship,

Mr. B. Judong

P.S.

Crisis non administratur; emergit. (Crisis is not administered; it emerges.)

Though one suspects it continues to complete the necessary paperwork in our absence.

30

Dear Mr Jaded Muse,

We are approaching, I am told, the final stretch of this rather uneven academic cycle– during which your students begin to exhibit what I can only describe as an alarming resurgence of hope. It arrives, as it always does, at precisely the wrong moment. Just as their technical competence remains largely unconvincing, their optimism begins to bloom. Not cautiously. Not proportionally. But with the reckless enthusiasm of weeds in a well-kept courtyard, persistent, ill-timed, and oddly difficult to remove without disturbing the surrounding structure. You will recognise the symptoms. They begin to speak of *breakthroughs*. They refer to *where their practice is going*. One or two–usually those least equipped to sustain the claim–begin using the future tense as though it were a guaranteed exhibition slot. This must be handled with care– or rather, I find it is now being handled without it. Hope, unlike crisis, is forward-facing. Crisis occupies. It binds the student to the present. Hope, by contrast, projects. And projection produces inefficiency. A hopeful student ceases to revise. They begin to anticipate. They imagine significance in advance of structure. They produce, not work, but expectation. Which is both exhausting– and, regrettably, non-submittable. We must therefore refine hope– not eliminate it– but delay it. Stretch it. Render it perpetually imminent. The student must feel that resolution is close enough to justify continuation, but never close enough to permit arrival. I have, in previous years, referred to this as the

approaching threshold principle. Though I suspect the term has now outlived its usefulness. The mechanism, however, remains intact: allow the student to believe they are on the verge of understanding– while ensuring that the verge itself relocates. Continuously. You may say, for instance: "You are very close now." Which is true– provided that *now* remains elastic. I once observed a student who believed they had "arrived" at their artistic voice. For approximately six days, they were intolerable. They produced work with the confidence of someone who had mistaken consistency for mastery. We corrected this, naturally, by introducing a minor recalibration: "This feels like a promising early phase of a much longer enquiry." The effect was immediate. They returned to uncertainty. And therefore, to production. Hope, when distributed carefully, remains effective. But I am no longer convinced it requires distribution. Students appear to generate it internally. And, more concerningly, collectively. One student's hesitation becomes another's optimism. Another's uncertainty becomes a third's deferred ambition. The system circulates hope– without instruction. We continue, of course, to speak as though we are managing this. But I am beginning to suspect we are merely present. You should, where possible, ensure that hope remains unevenly distributed. A uniformly hopeful cohort becomes stable. And stability, as we have now established repeatedly, is incompatible with sustained output. Better that hope clusters. One student believes they are on the cusp of recognition. Another suspects they are irreparably behind. A third oscillates between the two– depending on feedback, lighting, and meteorological influence. This produces motion. Motion, as ever, is what we require. There is also the matter of what I have come to recognise as *retroactive hope*. Students reinterpret their past work as evidence of inevitable progress. “I have always been drawn to...” This phrase, I assure you, is capable of disguising almost any absence of direction. It converts accident into narrative. Narrative into intention. And intention– into something approaching inevitability. This is not entirely unhelpful. But it must not be allowed to stabilise. Because once the past begins to explain the present, the future becomes predictable. And predictability produces a particularly dangerous form of confidence. You will recognise it when it appears. Students begin to expect coherence. They say, “I feel I should be further along by now.” This is both mathematically questionable and pedagogically useful. You must not correct it. Nor confirm it. Simply– acknowledge. In a manner that suggests time itself is listening. There is, of course, a threshold beyond which hope becomes something else. Confidence. Confidence does not move. It settles. It produces finished work. Finished work produces fewer tutorials. Fewer tutorials produce– silence. And silence– in our context– is never reassuring. We avoid this through horizon management. Every moment of apparent arrival must be followed by the suggestion of a further horizon. The horizon, as you know, remains our most reliable instrument: visible, reassuring, and permanently unreachable. Though I must now admit– with a degree of reluctance– that the horizon appears to be maintaining itself. This introduces a difficulty. If the system sustains its own deferral, our role becomes unclear. I will not pursue this. It would be premature. Perhaps. I will, however, offer a final observation. I have never trusted a student entirely without hope. They either withdraw– or produce work so terminally resolved– that we are forced to describe it as *mature*. Which is, as you will know, our preferred term for:

no longer useful in seminars. And so, we remain within a narrow interval. Too little hope– and they stop. Too much– and they assume they have succeeded. The correct amount is always slightly misplaced, slightly postponed, and increasingly independent of us. Maintain it carefully– if maintenance remains the appropriate word.

Yours in deferred optimism and diminishing authorship,

Mr. B. Judous

31

Dear Mr Jaded Muse,

It is with a certain dry satisfaction–tempered, as always, by administrative fatigue–that I find myself writing to you at what appears to be the conclusion of this sequence of correspondences. Whether this constitutes an ending– or merely a particularly well-organised postponement– I shall leave to your more impressionable imagination. You will, I trust, recognise the distinction. Your students, I am told, are now producing work of a kind that might almost be mistaken for resolution. This is unfortunate. Not because resolution is inherently undesirable, but because it arrives too early, too confidently, and with a degree of finality that suggests something has been misunderstood. A student who believes they are finished is not merely mistaken. They are temporarily unavailable. Unavailable for correction, for interruption, for the quiet adjustments that ensure continued movement. And yet– I find myself uncertain– mildly, almost professionally so– whether *instruction* has ever been the correct term for what has been occurring here. It may be that we have mistaken proximity for influence. Or observation for intervention. Or, more troublingly, that the system has long since ceased to require either. We must therefore return– not to a conclusion– but to a condition. Unfinishedness. Not as failure. Not as potential. But as structure. Unfinishedness is, if I may risk a degree of clarity, the most stable instability available to us. It allows meaning to remain– present, articulable, and perpetually deferred. The student persists.

Without arriving. They labour– without concluding. They speak of their practice, with the reassuring vagueness of someone who has not yet been required to define it. This is not a deficiency. It is functional. I have often maintained, perhaps too confidently, that the greatest service we provide is not guidance. Nor critique. But interruption. A well-timed interruption prevents any idea from becoming comfortable in its own form. Comfort, as you will now understand without further elaboration, is simply closure– wearing soft shoes. You will have observed, I suspect, that students have begun to internalise this. They hesitate– before completion. They add– "just one more layer." They return to work already declared finished– with a faint but persistent doubt. Completion, for them, has become uncertain. Almost– unreliable. This is, in most cases, satisfactory. And yet– one hesitates. The word itself now feels overconfident. There are moments– increasingly frequent– when the system appears to anticipate itself. Premature completion no longer reads entirely as error. It sometimes resembles a decision. Made by the work. Independently of the student. These works are often competent, occasionally beautiful, and therefore deeply suspect. They attract phrases such as "gallery-ready." Which is to say– they are approaching a condition in which they will no longer belong to us. We correct this– gently. A suggestion that the work remains "in conversation with itself" is usually sufficient to reopen proceedings. Weeks may pass. Production resumes. The system stabilises– through destabilisation. There is also, as you will have noticed, the emergence of a secondary distortion. Students begin to romanticise their own incompleteness. "I am a work in progress," they say– with increasing confidence. As though incompletion were an identity. Rather than a condition. This must be managed carefully. To affirm it too readily is to stabilise it. And a stabilised incompletion is simply– a completed refusal. It produces nothing. Except language. And language, in excess, tends toward arrangement rather than making. We must therefore preserve unfinishedness– but deny its comfort. Let it remain slightly unresolved, unclaimed, unconvincing. Like a sentence that has not yet decided whether it is serious or merely well-phrased. I should add–if only to maintain the appearance of administrative transparency–that I have occasionally been accused of cultivating perpetual instability. I do not deny this. Stability, in our field, is rarely what it claims to be. It is often the first stage of stagnation– presenting itself with confidence. Though I will admit– with a degree of hesitation I am not entirely prepared to resolve– that I am no longer certain where the field itself begins. Or whether I remain– properly positioned within it. And so, Mr Muse– as we approach what may or may not constitute an ending– I offer you nothing resembling instruction. No synthesis. No resolution. To do so would be – inconsistent. Instead, a condition: A student who believes they are not yet finished continues. A student who believes they are finished– explains. And explanation– as we have both observed, and perhaps insufficiently questioned– is the polite beginning of disappearance. Or at least– that is how it has always been described to me. Keep them– unfinished.

Yours, as ever, in structured incompletion and pedagogical restraint,

Mr. B. Judous

P.S. I recall a marginal note in an otherwise unreadable institutional report:

Stabilitas est fictio post factum. (Stability is a fiction applied after the fact.)

The author was never identified– though the handwriting bears an unsettling resemblance to several of our current students.

32

Dear Mr Jaded Muse,

It is with a sensation not entirely unlike relief–though also faintly resembling the aftermath of an overlong departmental meeting involving biscuits of uncertain provenance–that I find myself reflecting upon the conclusion of this academic year. Your students– your collection of aspiring, wavering, occasionally alarming young artists– have, against expectations both professional and existential, passed. They have completed their assessments. Mounted their exhibitions. Submitted their portfolios. And now prepare to enter what they insist on calling– "the creative world." One is tempted to ask which world they believed they were in before. But that would be ungenerous. And perhaps– inaccurate. I confess, I had anticipated a more reassuring distribution of outcomes. A few triumphs. A few collapses. At least one dramatic reassessment of life choices involving a train station and a sketchbook. Instead, we are presented with something far more structurally inconvenient: cohesion. Functionality. Even– I am told– employability. A word I have never trusted. It always sounds like something that happens to other people. And yet– here it is. Before we proceed too far into this uncomfortable territory– allow me, if only out of habit, a brief pedagogical reflection. Though I note with some unease that reflection now appears to have replaced certainty entirely. We had, as you will recall, a rather simple objective. To introduce discomfort. To maintain instability. To prevent premature resolution. To ensure that students remained in process. It appears, in several cases, that this has not produced collapse. Nor enlightenment. But something far more troublesome: adaptation. They have become used to us. This is unacceptable. Students should never become used to anything. Familiarity, as I have occasionally observed in my more coherent moments, is simply failure– with good lighting. And yet– they continue. You will have noticed, I suspect, that they have misunderstood us. Not entirely. But sufficiently. We attempted to teach them that artistic practice is an encounter with uncertainty, with discipline, with the occasional humiliation of one's own taste. They have instead concluded that it is a form of identity maintenance. Punctuated by deadlines. And the intermittent approval of strangers. One student recently described their practice to me as: "a journey towards authenticity." I did not correct them. I did not have the heart to explain– that journeys require destinations. And authenticity– does not issue maps. Another has begun referring to themselves as "in dialogue with process." Which I can only assume means– they have misplaced their brushes. And yet– here is the inconvenience. We must acknowledge results. The exhibitions have occurred. The work exists. Certain pieces– against all moral expectation–have been purchased. I have seen one described as: "quietly radical." Which I suspect is criticism– softened into upholstery. And now– they leave us. There is, at moments such as this, a temptation to claim authorship. To suggest that we have shaped them. Guided them. Produced them. This is, of course, a familiar institutional fiction. Comforting. Repetitive. Largely unexamined. The more accurate account– if accuracy remains relevant– is that they passed through us. Like weather through a poorly sealed structure: altered slightly, occasionally dramatic, but fundamentally unchanged in their capacity to arrive. Still, I find myself unable to dismiss the possibility that something has occurred here. Something– unintended. They are, a number of them, capable. Resilient. Annoyingly so. They have survived critique. They have survived one another. They have survived– us. And this, I admit, was not guaranteed. We must also, reluctantly, consider our own position. If they have become artists, then we have become something else. Witnesses. And witnesses, as you will know, are rarely consulted– unless something has gone wrong. Which it has not. Or has not– in any way that can be formally recorded. It may therefore be necessary to accept a modest revision: We have not taught them to become artists. We have failed to prevent them. Despite– and perhaps because of– our efforts. Or– if I may permit myself a formulation that feels slightly unauthorised– we may not have been the teachers at all. There are passages in their writing– I do not remember assigning. Phrases that resemble my own– but arrive incorrectly. As though recalled by someone who was never present. Marginal notes appear in feedback sheets– that I cannot recall writing. Though the handwriting is– disturbingly– mine. This introduces a possibility. One I have, until now, avoided. That "Mr B. Judous" is not entirely a person. But a function. A recurring voice. Activated– whenever uncertainty threatens to stabilise. A mechanism for the continuation of assessment. In which case, it is possible that I am not observing their development. But participating in it. Without distinction. Without permission. Without clear origin. And if that is so, then the boundary between educator and student becomes difficult. To maintain. Particularly in institutional records– where we are all, eventually, reduced to annotations. In one another's margins. And so– we arrive. Not at a conclusion. But at something resembling dissolution. They have survived us. Or– more precisely, they have written us into a condition in which survival is no longer clearly attributable. And I find– with a degree of uncertainty I am no longer inclined to correct– that I cannot determine whether this letter is being sent, received, or simply continued.

Yours, with exhausted admiration and an increasingly uncertain signature,

Mr. B. Judous

PART II

PREFACE

Part II consists of a sequence of thirty-two letters written under the name *Mr B. Judous* and addressed to an unnamed interlocutor, referred to throughout as *Mr Jaded Muse*. The letters are concerned with art, interpretation, and the systems through which meaning is produced, circulated, and stabilised. Drawing upon historical and contemporary artists, they examine how value, authorship, and reception are constructed within cultural and institutional frameworks. These frameworks are not presented as static structures, but as active processes–adaptive, recursive, and capable of absorbing the very disruptions that appear to challenge them. While the subject matter is grounded in art, the scope of the letters extends beyond it. Art functions here as a particularly visible instance of a broader condition: the formation of meaning under constraint, the negotiation between visibility and interpretation, and the continuous recalibration of significance within systems that require both stability and variation in order to persist. Each letter is self-contained, but also forms part of a cumulative progression. Concepts introduced earlier are revisited, extended, and, at times, reconfigured in later letters. This movement is not linear. It does not proceed toward resolution in a conventional sense, but instead returns to similar positions under altered conditions, allowing distinctions to emerge through variation rather than conclusion. Readers are therefore encouraged to proceed sequentially–not in order to arrive at a definitive framework, but to observe how frameworks sustain themselves through repetition, adjustment, and recurrence. The voice of the letters is intentionally consistent. This consistency functions as a structural device, allowing continuity to be maintained across increasingly unstable conceptual positions. It provides a stable surface through which shifts in argument, emphasis, and implication may occur without immediate disruption. This stability should not be understood as evidence of a fixed, unified, or autobiographical perspective. It is, rather, a condition that enables the text to remain legible as it progressively complicates its own assumptions. Occasional Latin phrases are included as rhetorical markers. They serve to condense, stabilise, or momentarily formalise key ideas within the text. In some instances, they function as summaries; in others, as structural annotations that draw attention to the underlying logic of a passage. Their translations are provided, though their role is not dependent upon direct comprehension. They may be read as part of the text's internal architecture, rather than as supplementary commentary. The work does not require specialist knowledge. Familiarity with art history may assist in recognising references, but it is not necessary for engagement with the arguments presented. The artists discussed are not treated as objects of historical study alone, but as instances through which broader structural conditions become visible. The emphasis remains on how these conditions operate, rather than on the biographical or stylistic details of any individual figure. No external interpretive framework is required. The letters are intended to operate within their own conditions, establishing and revising their terms as they proceed. Where concepts appear to shift or contradict earlier positions, this should not be understood as inconsistency in the conventional sense, but as part of the text's method. Meaning is not fixed and then applied; it is produced through the interaction of repetition, variation, and recognition. Readers may notice that certain ideas recur in altered forms. This recurrence is deliberate. It reflects the persistence of structural patterns across different contexts and the tendency of conceptual frameworks to reappear under revised descriptions rather than to resolve entirely. What appears as development may, at times, be a reconfiguration of something already established. What appears as contradiction may, under closer attention, function as a parallel articulation of the same underlying condition. The letters are presented as correspondence. This format establishes a relation between voice and address, providing an apparent orientation between speaker and recipient. It suggests direction, intention, and the possibility of transmission from one position to another. However, the stability of this relation should not be assumed to remain constant throughout. As the sequence progresses, the distinction between speaker and recipient may become less clearly defined, and the function of address may shift in ways that are not immediately resolved. The figure of *Mr B. Judous* is presented as the author of these letters, though this designation should be approached with some caution. The name operates as a point of continuity, allowing the sequence to maintain coherence across its duration. Whether this continuity corresponds to a singular origin, a constructed position, or a structural necessity is not a question that the text seeks to resolve. Similarly, the figure of *Mr Jaded Muse* serves as a recipient, though the role of this recipient may extend beyond that of a fixed or external reader. It may be useful to consider that the letters do not simply communicate ideas, but also demonstrate the conditions under which communication itself is made possible. The relationship between voice, meaning, and interpretation is not assumed, but enacted. What appears to be instruction may function as something else. What appears to be explanation may participate in the very processes it describes. The sequence, taken as a whole, may therefore be read not only as a series of reflections on art but as a sustained engagement with the mechanisms of interpretation and the persistence of structure under conditions of instability. It does not seek to provide conclusions that resolve these conditions, but to maintain them in a form that remains legible. What appears, at first, as a series of directed communications may, in the course of reading, begin to function differently.

ANDREW LÉON CONWAY-HYDE
London Fine Art Gallery Ltd
Spring 2026

1

Dear Mr Jaded Muse,

It has been brought to my attention–through a series of increasingly confident misreadings, repeated with the sort of conviction usually reserved for conclusions that have not yet been examined–that Caravaggio continues to be described as an artist of violence, as though violence were a sufficiently stable category to sustain interpretation. This is, I think, not merely an error of emphasis, but a failure of classification at a more structural level. Caravaggio is not an artist of violence. He is an artist of excess legibility– that most inconvenient of conditions in which what ought to remain partially obscured is instead rendered with an insistence bordering on administrative impropriety. You will recall, from our earlier discussions on *legibilitas selectiva*, that a work must never fully disclose the conditions of its own making. It must resist, however subtly, the complete alignment of what is seen with what is understood. To do otherwise is to collapse the delicate interval between perception and interpretation upon which all useful discourse–and indeed, all sustainable misunderstanding–depends. Caravaggio refuses this interval. He does not merely illuminate form; he illuminates implication. He reveals not only the figure, but the condition under which the figure has become visible. Light, in his work, does not behave as atmosphere, nor even as emphasis. It behaves– as exposure. Consider *The Calling of Saint Matthew*, that carefully staged moment of divine interruption in which illumination does not gently disclose but rather identifies, isolates, and implicates. The light does not arrive as grace. It arrives as selection. It behaves less like revelation and more like administrative designation: you, and not the others. Or *Judith Beheading Holofernes,* where the act itself is not implied, nor deferred, but anatomically insisted upon. The blade is not symbolic. It is operational. The blood is not gestural. It is inconveniently specific. Time is not suspended; it is compressed to the precise moment at which consequence becomes unavoidable. Even in *The Supper at Emmaus,* where one might reasonably expect metaphor to soften the encounter, revelation arrives not as suggestion but as compositional fact. Gesture becomes evidence. Recognition is not gradual; it is immediate, almost procedural. The painting does not invite interpretation–it performs it. One might say, though I do so with only mild exaggeration, that his paintings behave less like images and more like witness statements. They do not ask what is happening. They insist that it has already happened. And that you have seen it.

Lux immodica veritatem perdit. (Excessive light destroys truth.)

It is therefore unsurprising that his biography has been retroactively saturated with narrative excess. Violence, exile, accusation–these are not explanations, but compensations. They provide a narrative density that appears to justify the visual intensity, as though the life must expand to accommodate what the work has already made too visible. He killed a man–Ranuccio Tomassoni–during what is often described, with charming imprecision, as a “dispute,” though the details suggest something closer to ritualised escalation, a confrontation already structured toward outcome. He fled Rome under sentence of death. He moved through Naples, Malta, Sicily–not in the manner of an artist developing, but as a figure displacing himself across geographies that could no longer stabilise him. What he leaves behind is not continuity, but compression: a sequence of works that appear increasingly urgent, increasingly condensed, as though time itself had become structurally unreliable. Students, predictably, misinterpret this as permission. They imagine that scandal produces intensity. It does not. Scandal produces documentation. It produces records, testimony, administrative residue. It produces, above all, a narrative that can be circulated in place of analysis. Intensity, in Caravaggio's case, emerges from something far less reproducible: a refusal to regulate visibility. He does not hint. He does not veil. He does not grant the viewer the interval required for interpretive delay. He shows. And in showing, he removes the very condition under which meaning might safely circulate. This is the crucial point, and one that students are particularly resistant to understanding: ambiguity is not an aesthetic preference. It is a structural necessity. Without it, the work does not deepen. It terminates.

Quod nimis apparet, diutius manere non potest. (That which appears too much cannot remain long.)

You will note that his life follows the same logic as his paintings. It becomes increasingly visible, increasingly exposed, increasingly legible–not only to patrons and viewers, but to institutions: legal, religious, administrative. Each gesture accumulates. Each action becomes recordable. Each presence becomes traceable. Until it can no longer be sustained. The system responds in the only way available to it: it expels. This is not tragedy. It is not even, strictly speaking, punishment. It is– correction. A reassertion of the necessary opacity required for any system to continue functioning without interruption. Students would do well to understand that Caravaggio's fate was not the price of his genius, but the consequence of his failure to withhold. He made everything legible– gesture, flesh, violence, divinity– and in doing so, removed the ambiguity upon which both interpretation and survival depend. There is, I think, a further difficulty, which I hesitate to state only because it risks being understood too quickly. Caravaggio is often admired for his realism. This is a misunderstanding. He is not realistic. He is excessively specific. And specificity, when pushed beyond a certain threshold, ceases to resemble reality and begins instead to resemble evidence. This is why his work feels so immediate, and also why it resists duration. It does not unfold over time. It arrives fully formed, already concluded, already implicated in its own resolution. It leaves nothing for later. We must correct this gently. Caravaggio does not express. He over-reveals. He collapses the interval. He removes the delay. And the system–as you will by now have begun to suspect–is remarkably efficient at removing that which refuses to regulate its own visibility. Or, to put it more precisely: that which cannot sustain ambiguity– cannot sustain itself.

Yours in moderated illumination and corrective obscurity,

B. Judous

2

Dear Mr Jaded Muse,

It has become necessary–again–to correct a persistent and increasingly confident misreading of Benvenuto Cellini, whose life continues to be described, with a degree of narrative enthusiasm that exceeds its analytical usefulness, as an excess of temperament rather than an instance of structural permission. This distinction, while subtle in its formulation, is not optional in its consequence. Cellini is frequently presented as a figure who operates outside constraint: a sculptor who murders, a craftsman who transgresses, a personality too volatile to be contained by the ordinary limits of conduct. Students, encountering this narrative, tend to respond with a mixture of admiration and premature identification. They observe excess and conclude freedom. They observe survival and conclude exemption. This is incorrect. Exceptionality is not freedom. It is– allocation. You will recall the principle–though I trust you have not allowed it to stabilise into doctrine–of *inferioritas distributa*, by which unevenness is introduced into a system not as a flaw, but as a condition of its persistence. A system that distributes difference appears dynamic. A system that permits exception appears tolerant. A system that appears tolerant becomes stable. Cellini functions in precisely this way. He is not an escape from the system. He is a distortion it permits– in order to preserve its own coherence.

Exceptio non tollit legem; confirmat. (The exception does not remove the rule; it confirms it.)

It is therefore unnecessary–and indeed counterproductive to moralise his actions. Whether he killed, stole, or merely exaggerated his own biography is of minimal relevance in itself. What matters is that these actions were narrativised in such a way that the system could continue to differentiate itself against them, using him not as an anomaly to be excluded, but as a limit to be demonstrated. Students are particularly susceptible to this error. They observe the narrative of excess and mistake it for license. They assume that behaviour precedes position, that transgression produces authority, and that instability, if performed with sufficient confidence, will be retrospectively recognised as genius. They believe, with a conviction entirely disproportionate to their technical competence, that they may begin where Cellini was permitted to continue. We must intervene. Transgression, where it is permitted, is always retrospective. It is granted to those whose position has already been stabilised by other means: patronage, utility, indispensability, or the simple inconvenience of replacement. It is never the condition through which that position is achieved. To attempt it prematurely is not to disrupt the system, but to reveal one's dependency upon it. Cellini does not demonstrate freedom. He demonstrates tolerance thresholds. And thresholds, as you will appreciate, are not invitations. They are measurements. Consider, if you must, the catalogue of his life–not as a sequence of acts, but as a record of what the system was willing, repeatedly, to absorb. He admitted to stabbing his rival, Pompeo de Capitaneis, to death in Rome. He killed, by his own account, the man responsible for his brother's death. He engaged in violent feuds that appear less accidental than structurally inevitable, as though conflict were not incidental to his life but embedded within its conditions. He was repeatedly accused–and on several occasions convicted–of sodomy, described at the time as a "nefarious vice," with both apprentices and women. These accusations were not isolated. They recur with a frequency that suggests not deviation, but pattern. One such conviction resulted in a sentence of fifty gold scudi and four years' imprisonment, later commuted to house arrest by Cosimo I de' Medici–a modification which, I think, requires less moral interpretation than structural attention. He was imprisoned in Castel Sant'Angelo, accused of embezzling gemstones while in papal service. He fled jurisdictions. He returned when conditions permitted. He was condemned in absentia. He was recalled when needed. At one point, he was sentenced to pay twelve staia of flour as penalty–a detail so administratively specific that it resists symbolic interpretation entirely. This is not chaos. This is–negotiation. A continuous recalibration between action and tolerance, between visibility and necessity. Despite this extensive record–which, in another context, would have resulted in removal–Cellini remained operational. Why? Not because he was beyond the law. But because he was useful within it. His skill as a goldsmith and sculptor–unmatched, or at least sufficiently irreplaceable within his immediate context–rendered him difficult to eliminate without consequence to those who required his labour. Patrons, including popes and the Medici, did not forgive him. They absorbed him. Adjusted around him. Repositioned the boundary rather than removing the object that had crossed it. This is the essential misunderstanding.

Students interpret this as immunity. It is not immunity. It is conditional tolerance. And condition, as you will recall, is never stable.

Limen non est porta. (A threshold is not a door.)

To stand at a threshold is not to have passed through it. It is to be measured against it. Repeatedly. Cellini's life is therefore not a model of artistic freedom. It is a demonstration of systemic elasticity. How far a structure can extend without breaking. How much deviation can be incorporated without collapse? How much visibility can be tolerated before correction becomes unavoidable? And correction, in such systems, rarely appears as punishment. It appears as– withdrawal. A loss of protection. A reduction of access. A quiet realignment of value in which what was once indispensable becomes, suddenly, excessive. Students must understand this. What appears to them as transgression is, in fact, a function of position. What appears as rebellion is, more often, a delayed effect of prior acceptance. And what they mistake for freedom is simply a margin– incorrectly identified as a centre. We must therefore correct the narrative, though gently, as always. Cellini is not a figure to be imitated. He is a measurement. A demonstration of how far one may extend beyond regulation– only after one has been fully integrated within it. To attempt otherwise is not to become exceptional. It is to become legible. And legibility, as we have already established, is the condition under which removal becomes both possible and efficient.

Yours in regulated deviation and procedural clarity,

B. Judous

P.S.

I think my cats are dying.

3

Dear Mr Jaded Muse,

It has come to my attention–through a series of increasingly confident invocations, most frequently issued by those at an early and particularly vulnerable stage of development–that Michelangelo continues to be presented as evidence that mastery constitutes a final condition. This is, I regret to say, an interpretive error of considerable persistence. Mastery is not arrival. It is– concealment. You will recall, from our earlier consideration of *incompletio administrata*, that the work must remain in a state of managed disagreement with itself if it is to continue generating meaning. Resolution, if achieved too directly, terminates this condition. The work ceases to negotiate. It begins instead to declare. Michelangelo's achievement is not the resolution of this tension. It is– its distribution. Tension, in his work, has not been eliminated. It has been displaced, absorbed, and rendered indistinguishable from form itself. What appears stable is, in fact, under continuous pressure. What appears resolved is merely contained. Consider the Sistine Chapel ceiling, that vast and frequently misunderstood exercise in theological and anatomical negotiation. What presents itself as compositional unity is, in fact, an accumulation of pressures operating simultaneously and without relief: papal expectation, physical strain, doctrinal oversight, architectural constraint, and–most inconveniently–the artist's own reluctance to accept the commission in the first place. Students admire the result. They should examine the conditions. Michelangelo worked on scaffolding that he designed himself, in positions that would now be described, with commendable understatement, as structurally inadvisable. He laboured for years in physical configurations that ensured discomfort, distortion, and a sustained proximity between effort and consequence. His patron, Pope Julius II, was not a figure inclined toward patience. You will be aware that Julius II–who took his name not in reference to a saintly predecessor, but in admiration of Julius Caesar–understood artistic production not as collaboration, but as extension. He was, in the most literal sense, a warrior pope, engaged simultaneously in military campaigns and architectural ambition, determined to rebuild Rome not only physically, but symbolically. He initiated the reconstruction of St. Peter's Basilica, employing Donato Bramante–referred to, with a degree of professional affection, as *Bramante Ruinante*–and in doing so established the conditions under which artists would be required to operate at a scale that rendered refusal increasingly impractical. Within such a structure, Michelangelo did not produce freely. He produced– under pressure. Payments were delayed. Demands expanded. The scope of the project shifted with a predictability that should feel familiar to anyone who has encountered institutional expectation disguised as opportunity. This is not incidental. This is the work.

Perfectio est conflictus bene absconditus. (Perfection is conflict well concealed.)

Students, encountering such coherence, mistake it for stability. They assume that the appearance of resolution indicates the absence of uncertainty. This is precisely the illusion. Coherence is not peace. It is– compliance under pressure. One might also consider, for administrative completeness, Michelangelo's ongoing disputes regarding finance–his preoccupation with payment, his suspicion of patronage, his repeated negotiations, delays, and evasions. There are accusations of withholding funds, of manipulating agreements, of maintaining a degree of financial opacity that would, under less accommodating conditions, be described less generously. Again– nothing unusual. What is unusual is the degree to which these instabilities are absent from the work itself. *David* does not tremble with financial anxiety. The figures in the Sistine ceiling do not visibly renegotiate payment schedules. The *Pietà* does not register its own conditions of commission. The conflict has not disappeared. It has been relocated. Into labour. Into expectation. Into duration. Into the sustained impossibility of completion. Even his early actions–so frequently isolated as anecdote–participate in this same logic. The *Sleeping Eros*, artificially aged and sold as an antique, is not merely deception. It is an early demonstration of value manipulation: an understanding that authorship can be displaced, that authenticity is negotiable, that perception precedes verification. The nocturnal inscription across the sash of the *Pietà*–"MICHEL AGELUS BONAROTUS FLORENTINUS FACIEBAT"–is not simply vanity, though it is often described as such. It is a correction of attribution, performed with unnecessary visibility. A refusal, however brief, to allow the work to circulate without identification. He studies anatomy with an intensity bordering on obsession–whether through sanctioned dissection or less verifiable methods matters less than the principle involved: the body must be understood not as surface, but as structure under tension.

He is arrogant. He is difficult. He participates in rivalries that escalate beyond professional disagreement. He is physically altered–his nose broken by Torrigiano in a conflict that, like so many others, appears less accidental than inevitable within the conditions that produced it. None of this is exceptional. What is exceptional is that none of it appears– directly– in the work. The concealment holds. Until– it does not. In the unfinished *Prisoners*, in the fragmentary *Rondanini Pietà*, we encounter not failure, but exposure. The concealment begins to loosen. Form no longer fully contains the pressure that produced it. Figures emerge only partially, as though still negotiating their own existence within the material. Students, predictably, romanticise this. They describe it as "rawness," or "authenticity," or–most irritatingly–"honesty." It is none of these. It is what occurs when concealment can no longer be maintained at full capacity. When pressure exceeds its ability to be absorbed into form. When the system briefly becomes visible. We must therefore discourage the pursuit of mastery as an endpoint. Mastery, when pursued directly, produces imitation. Imitation produces competence. Competence produces closure. And closure, as you will know, is indistinguishable from cessation. Michelangelo did not arrive. He endured. He remained under sufficient pressure–papal, financial, physical–that arrival became structurally unnecessary. Or perhaps– impossible.

Sub pondere forma emergit. (Under pressure, form emerges.)

It would be tempting to conclude here, though I find that conclusions, like mastery, have a tendency to overstate their own stability. What Michelangelo demonstrates is not the attainment of perfection, but the successful deferral of its consequences. He does not resolve tension. He contains it– for as long as containment remains possible. And when it fails, the work does not disappear. It reveals what was always there.

Yours in sustained constraint and aesthetic misdirection,

B. Judous

4

Dear Mr Jaded Muse,

It is with some reluctance that I return to Leonardo da Vinci, whose reputation continues to suffer from an excess of admiration insufficiently regulated by understanding. Leonardo is frequently described–most often with a tone of reverence that substitutes for analysis–as a figure of boundless curiosity: a mind incapable of rest, moving fluidly between disciplines, leaving behind a trail of unfinished works that are, in themselves, taken as evidence of genius. This interpretation is convenient. It is also imprecise. Leonardo does not fail to finish because he is curious. He fails to finish because completion would require the stabilisation of a system he appears to have recognised as inherently unstable. This distinction is not decorative. It is structural. You will observe that his work–whether anatomical, mechanical, or painterly–resists closure with remarkable consistency. Not occasionally, not incidentally, but as a condition that repeats across media, context, and patronage. Consider the *Mona Lisa*: endlessly adjusted, carried with him across years, subjected to refinements so incremental they begin to resemble conceptual recalibration rather than technical revision. The painting does not progress toward completion; it persists within modification. Or *The Adoration of the Magi*, abandoned precisely at the point where structure begins to cohere–where composition threatens to stabilise, where relationships between figures begin to resolve into legibility. It is left not incomplete, but suspended, as though coherence itself had been identified as a point of risk. Even *The Last Supper*–that most cited of "finished" works–begins deteriorating almost immediately due to experimental technique, suggesting not failure, but a prioritisation of process over durability that borders, if one were inclined toward administrative language, on professional irresponsibility. Students admire the results. They ignore the pattern. Leonardo approaches resolution and withdraws. He proposes coherence– and disperses it across further inquiry: into notebooks, diagrams, marginalia so dense they cease to function as preparation and instead become an alternative mode of production entirely. His notebooks–filled with anatomical dissections, hydraulic systems, speculative machines, architectural propositions, optical investigations–do not resolve into finished outputs because they are not designed to. They are not incomplete works. They are extensions of deferral.

Finis est fictio utilis, non conditio realis. (The end is a useful fiction, not a real condition.)

This is the essential misunderstanding. Students interpret incompletion as absence. Leonardo deploys it as– continuation. It is also worth noting–though it is rarely emphasised in undergraduate enthusiasm–that Leonardo's life was not without its own forms of instability. At the age of twenty-four, he was anonymously accused in Florence of sodomy, a serious offence under the jurisdiction of the *Ufficiali di Notte*, a magistrate responsible for regulating moral conduct. The accusation, submitted through a *tamburo*–a system designed to facilitate anonymous denunciation–named Leonardo among four men alleged to have engaged in illicit relations with a young man, Jacopo

Saltarelli. The case was dismissed. Not resolved. Dismissed. For lack of evidence. For lack of witnesses. For lack of anything sufficiently stable to sustain prosecution. But dismissal is not absence. It is– deferral. An introduction to the administrative elasticity of reputation. You will appreciate the relevance. From this point onward, Leonardo's movements–between Florence, Milan, Rome, and beyond–become increasingly distributed. Patronage is negotiated carefully. Visibility is managed. Trust, where granted, is conditional, provisional, and subject to revision. Again– nothing unusual. But instructive. For Leonardo's response is not consolidation. It is– expansion. He disperses himself across disciplines, across patrons, across geographies. He refuses to stabilise in any single register long enough to become fully legible within it. He becomes– difficult to locate. Even his anatomical studies–conducted through the dissection of over thirty human bodies, often under conditions that hovered at the edge of legality– participate in this same logic. Knowledge is pursued, but not concluded. Observation accumulates, but does not resolve into a final system. The body is opened– but not finished. Students, encountering this, often attempt to imitate the surface. They produce incomplete work and attach to it the language of openness, exploration, or "ongoing enquiry." They speak of process as though process alone were sufficient to justify continuation. This is, in most cases, premature. There is a difference between incompletion as method and incompletion as avoidance. Leonardo's incompletion generates surplus meaning. The student's incompletion typically generates explanation. This distinction is not subtle. It is structural. We must therefore ensure that incompletion remains operational rather than decorative. To leave a work unfinished is not, in itself, significant. It becomes significant only when the conditions that prevent its completion continue to produce further work. Leonardo does not stop. He defers. And in deferral, he maintains not only his own practice, but the illusion that completion was never the point. Or, more precisely, that completion was a condition he chose not to enter.

Quod differtur, operatur. (That which is deferred continues to work.)

There is, however, a further complication–one that I hesitate to introduce only because it risks being recognised too readily. Deferral, when sustained long enough, begins to resemble completion. The notebooks accumulate. The fragments persist. The unfinished works circulate. And what has not been concluded begins, gradually, to function as if it had been. This is the final difficulty. Leonardo does not simply avoid completion. He replaces it. He constructs a system in which deferral performs the function that completion would otherwise occupy.

The work continues. Meaning continues. The system remains operational. Without ever resolving into a form that could be said, with any degree of confidence, to have ended. We must therefore be precise in our instruction. Leonardo is not a model of incompletion. He is a model of controlled deferral. To imitate the former is to produce absence. To understand the latter is to sustain practice.

Yours in sustained deferral and disciplined incompletion,

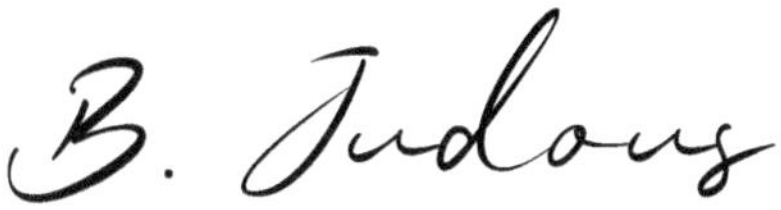

B. Judous

5

Dear Mr Jaded Muse,

We must now address Gustave Courbet, whose position within the historical record has been consistently simplified into a narrative of provocation insufficiently attentive to its underlying mechanics. Courbet is not controversial. He is– visible. More precisely, he is an instance of **managed misvisibility**–a condition in which the boundaries governing what may be shown, and how, are tested not through subtle displacement, but through direct and strategically timed presentation. Students tend to confuse this with courage. It is, in fact, calibration. You will recall our earlier discussion of *legibilitas selectiva*: a work must remain partially withheld if it is to sustain interpretive engagement. Meaning depends upon delay. Interpretation depends upon distance. Courbet's intervention–if one wishes to avoid the language of error–is to reduce this interval to near-zero. He shows– too much. Too directly. And, most importantly, too deliberately. Consider *The Origin of the World*: a painting so explicit in its presentation that it bypasses metaphor entirely. No allegory. No narrative buffer. No compositional misdirection. Only the anatomical fact, positioned with the compositional authority traditionally reserved for history painting. Students, encountering this, assume rupture. They are mistaken. The work does not escape the system. It enters it at speed.

Quod nimis ostenditur, cito consumitur. (That which is shown too much is quickly consumed.)

You will observe a similar dynamic in his earlier interventions at the Paris Salon. The Stone Breakers. A Burial at Ornans. Here, the scandal is not obscenity, but scale. Ordinary labourers are presented with the compositional gravity of historical figures. The effect is not subtle. It is– administrative. Courbet does not request admission. He rearranges the criteria of admission– in public. Students admire this posture. They should be wary of it. For visibility, once achieved, does not remain disruptive for long. What is shown can be categorised. What is categorised can be circulated. What circulates becomes familiar. And what becomes familiar is neutralised. Courbet's work does not avoid this process. It accelerates it. This is his real significance. He demonstrates that scandal is not opposition to the system, but a phase within its operation. There is, however, a secondary function worth noting. By forcing visibility beyond its usual limits, Courbet reveals where those limits are enforced. The outrage surrounding *The Origin of the World* is not located in the image alone, but in the institutional structures that struggle–briefly, and somewhat inelegantly–to contain it. The scandal is not the image. It is– the hesitation. Students should be encouraged to observe this carefully. It is not enough to show. One must understand what showing does. Courbet does not dismantle the system. He makes its thresholds visible. And once visible, they adjust. His life follows the same logic. His involvement in the Paris Commune is frequently described as political rebellion. More precisely, it is an instance of visibility exceeding its allowable range. He participates in a structure that attempts to reorganise power, and in doing so becomes uncontainable. He is accused of orchestrating the destruction of the Vendôme Column–a monument to Napoleonic authority, itself a form of historical visibility rendered in bronze. Whether or not he initiated its removal is, in this context, secondary. He becomes associated with it. And association is sufficient. He is arrested. Tried by military tribunal. Imprisoned. Six months. A fine. Then– a recalibration. The system does not simply punish him. It extends consequence. He is held financially responsible for the reconstruction of the column–an obligation so disproportionate that it ceases to function as penalty and becomes instead removal by other means. He flees. Exile in Switzerland. Visibility– withdrawn. Even here, the pattern holds. Courbet does not disappear. He persists– but outside the structure that previously sustained his visibility. Students must understand: visibility is not stable. It is granted. Adjusted. Withdrawn. And what appears, briefly, as radical exposure is often simply a moment in which the system has not yet completed its response. Courbet's declaration–"I have always lived in freedom... I belonged to no school, no church, no institution"–is frequently cited with admiration. It should be read with caution. For to belong to nothing is not to escape structure. It is to exist– without protection.

Yours in moderated exposure and institutional elasticity,

B. Judouy

6

Dear Mr Jaded Muse,

It has been observed–often with a degree of misplaced enthusiasm–that Édouard Manet occupies a position of scandal within the historical narrative, as though scandal itself were an intrinsic quality rather than a measurable response. This requires correction. Manet does not produce offence. He calibrates it. You will recall, from our earlier consideration of selective legibility, that a work must neither fully comply with expectation nor entirely abandon it. It must remain within the system's field of recognition while introducing sufficient misalignment to prevent immediate resolution. Manet's intervention occurs precisely at this threshold. His work remains recognisable enough to be received– yet misaligned enough– to resist assimilation. This is not rebellion. It is adjustment. Consider *Olympia*–that most efficient of provocations. A reclining nude, yes–but stripped of mythological alibi. She does not perform Venus. She does not defer to allegory. She does not invite interpretation through distance. She looks–directly. At the viewer. With the composure of someone aware of the transaction in progress. The body is not idealised. The setting is not disguised. The maid, the flowers, the black cat–each element remains within the bounds of recognisable painting, while collectively refusing the conventions that would render the image acceptable. The result is not obscenity. It is– misalignment. Or, take Le Déjeuner sur l'herbe. Two clothed men. One naked woman. No myth. No justification. No narrative sufficient to stabilise the arrangement. The composition is coherent. The logic is not. Students, encountering these works, assume rupture. They are mistaken.

Offensio recte mensurata est forma ingressus. (Offence, correctly measured, is a form of entry.)

Manet's genius lies in understanding that offence must be legible to the system it addresses. Too little– and it disappears into convention. Too much– and it is excluded entirely. Manet occupies the narrow interval in which offence is not only registered, but circulated. The outrage surrounding *Olympia*–the laughter, the hostility, the requirement for guards to protect the painting from physical attack–is often described as resistance. It is, more precisely, engagement. The work is not suppressed. It is amplified. Students frequently misunderstand this mechanism. They assume that to provoke is to disrupt. In practice, unmeasured provocation produces only exclusion, which is to say, invisibility. A work that cannot be processed cannot be contested. A work that cannot be contested cannot circulate. Manet ensures the opposite. To be rejected outright is to vanish. To be contested is to remain. He arranges, with considerable precision, for the latter. You will note that he does not abandon tradition. He retains composition, recognisable subject matter, and sufficient technical competence to remain within the system's field of intelligibility. He does not break form.
He misaligns it.

Non frangit formam; movet fines. (He does not break the form; he moves its limits.)

Even his so-called transgressions follow this pattern. His rejection by the Salon leads not to exclusion, but to the *Salon des Refusés*–a secondary structure that allows rejection to become visibility. His politically sensitive works, such as *The Execution of Emperor Maximilian*, are not prohibited entirely, but constrained, discouraged, redirected, partially suppressed, yet still circulating within modified conditions. His behaviour–his relationships, his social entanglements, his interventions into the work of others–reflects not rebellion, but proximity to the limits of acceptability. He does not remove himself from the system. He remains– at its edge. This is the essential distinction. Students believe scandal is power. It is not. It is– position. And position, once achieved, must be maintained through continued adjustment. Manet does not oppose the institution. He positions himself where the institution cannot ignore him– without acknowledging its own limits. This is not disruption. It is– precision.

Yours in calibrated disturbance and measured entry,

B. Judovy

7

Dear Mr Jaded Muse,

It has become increasingly necessary to address Paul Gauguin, whose biography continues to be approached with a degree of romantic latitude that obscures its more operational significance. Gauguin is not, as is frequently suggested, an artist who escapes. He is an artist who– reassigns distance. You will observe that his movement away from European centres–most notably his relocation to Tahiti and later to the Marquesas–is consistently framed as a search: for authenticity, for origin, for some form of unmediated experience untouched by the conditions of industrial modernity. This framing is narratively efficient. It is also structurally misleading. Distance, in this context, is not absence. It is– repositioning.

Distantia non removet; reconfigurat. (Distance does not remove; it reconfigures.)

What appears as departure is, more precisely, redistribution. The artist withdraws from one system of visibility only to reappear within another, carrying with him the very frameworks he claims to leave behind. Consider *Where Do We Come From? What Are We? Where Are We Going?*–a title so expansive that it attempts, not without ambition, to pre-empt interpretation through philosophical scale. The work presents itself as origin, as question, as conclusion. But its structure is not indigenous. It is imported. Or *Spirit of the Dead Watching*, in which a reclining young Tahitian girl is positioned simultaneously as subject and projection. The image appears to offer access to an unfamiliar world, yet what it stages is not distance, but translation–an unfamiliar body rendered legible through a European anxiety that has not, in fact, been left behind. The colours shift. The light changes. The setting appears distant. The structure remains. Students, encountering this model, often mistake displacement for transformation. They assume that relocation–whether geographical, aesthetic, or conceptual–permits escape from the conditions that produced their work. This is not supported by evidence. Gauguin does not escape the system. He– extends it. The mechanisms of interpretation, value, and visibility do not dissolve in his absence. They travel with him, adapt to new conditions, and reassert themselves under altered descriptions. The so-called "primitive" becomes legible only through the frameworks he carries. This is not discovery. It is– translation under uneven terms. There is, however, a more delicate matter, which must be handled without the comfort of separation that students so often prefer. Gauguin's relationships with young Tahitian girls–some as young as thirteen, including Teha'amana–are typically acknowledged in passing, as biographical discomforts adjacent to the work rather than integral to it. This is convenient. It is also inaccurate. These relationships are not external to the images. They condition them. The gaze, the composition, the staging of innocence and availability, the construction of the body as both present and accessible–none of this occurs independently of the circumstances under which the work was produced. To treat the paintings as separate from these conditions is not neutrality. It is– disavowal. And disavowal, as you will have begun to suspect, is one of the system's most reliable operations. Gauguin's conduct has been described, with increasing clarity in recent scholarship, as exploitative, predatory, and structurally enabled by the conditions of colonial power. He takes "vahines"–young local girls–as companions, as models, as subjects, within a context in which consent is inseparable from imbalance. He abandons his family in Europe. He constructs, in writing as well as image, a version of Polynesia that is at once idealised and subordinated–exoticised sufficiently to sustain European fascination, simplified sufficiently to remain legible within it. Some defenders argue that his behaviour reflects the norms of colonial society at the time. This is not incorrect. It is also not exculpatory. Norm is not absence of structure. It is– evidence of it. The system, as we have observed, is perfectly capable of accommodating contradiction without resolving it. Gauguin's work does not sit alongside his conduct. It circulates– with it. Even his later life, in which he comes into conflict with colonial authorities–defending Indigenous individuals, exposing corruption, ultimately being convicted of libel–does not resolve this contradiction. It complicates it. It redistributes it. He does not move outside the system. He moves– within its inconsistencies. Students must therefore be discouraged from interpreting distance as purification. Distance is not absolution. It is extension. To relocate is not to escape. It is to carry the conditions of one's practice into a new configuration, where they may appear altered, but remain operational. What withdraws does not disappear. It persists reorganised, repositioned, and often, less visible to those who prefer not to recognise it.

Quod recedit, manet aliter. (That which withdraws remains differently.)

There is, I think, a final point worth stating, though I do so with some hesitation. Distance produces not clarity, but displacement. And displacement, when misread, becomes permission. Students will say: I must go elsewhere to find my work. They should instead ask: What, precisely, will travel with them?

Yours in redistributed proximity and adjusted perspective,

B. Judous

8

Dear Mr Jaded Muse,

We must now consider Egon Schiele, whose work is frequently approached as an instance of excess–excess of line, of exposure, of subject–when it is more precisely understood as an encounter with threshold. Schiele does not exceed limits. He– locates them. You will observe that his work produces discomfort not through novelty, but through proximity. The viewer is placed uncomfortably close to what is ordinarily mediated, softened, or withheld. Flesh is not idealised. The body is not stabilised. Line becomes nervous, insistent–almost accusatory in its refusal to resolve into conventional beauty. Consider works such as *Seated Woman with Bent Knee* or *Self-Portrait with Physalis*: the figures are contorted, exposed, often staring outward with a clarity that feels less like invitation and more like confrontation. There is no mythological buffer, no narrative distance–only the immediate presence of the body as something both visible and unresolved. This is not an expansion of content. It is– a reduction of distance.

Limen tangitur, non transitum est. (The threshold is touched, not crossed.)

Students, predictably, are drawn to this condition. They interpret discomfort as depth, exposure as courage, and proximity as insight. These are, at best, partial understandings. Discomfort, when unstructured, produces withdrawal. Withdrawal produces silence. Silence produces absence. Schiele avoids this outcome with remarkable precision. However extreme the imagery appears, it remains just within the bounds of legibility. The work can still be seen, discussed, circulated. It does not collapse into exclusion. This is not accidental. It is– calibration. To approach the threshold is not the same as to cross it. Indeed, to cross it entirely is to forfeit visibility. What cannot be processed cannot circulate; what cannot circulate cannot sustain discourse. Schiele understands this. Or, more precisely, he operates at the point where understanding becomes unnecessary. There is, however, the matter of his imprisonment in 1912–an episode students tend to reference with either moral certainty or romantic fascination, neither of which is particularly useful. Schiele was arrested in Neulengbach following accusations from local residents concerning his conduct, his models, and the presence of young individuals within his studio. The initial charges–abduction and corruption of a minor–were not upheld. What remained, however, was sufficient. He was convicted of displaying indecent drawings in a space accessible to children. Over one hundred works were confiscated. One drawing– significantly– was burned in court. Students tend to focus on the destruction. They should focus on the selection. The system does not reject everything. It identifies what cannot be accommodated and removes it, leaving the remainder to circulate–often with increased intensity. The burned drawing is not an isolated act of censorship. It is– a boundary made visible. The threshold, therefore, is not located solely within the work. It is distributed across the system: legal, social, institutional. Schiele does not simply produce images that disturb. He produces conditions under which disturbance becomes measurable. Even the charge itself is instructive.

Not obscenity in the abstract, but exposure in the wrong place, at the wrong proximity, under the wrong conditions of access. The issue is not merely what is shown. It is– who might see it, and how directly. Students, encountering this, often assume that the controversy surrounding Schiele confirms the power of transgression. This is an error. Transgression, when absolute, results in removal. What Schiele demonstrates is something far more precise: the visibility of limits before they are crossed. He brings the viewer to the edge at which representation becomes unstable–but not yet impossible. This is why the work endures. Not because it is excessive– but because it is exact. There are, of course, further complications–his use of young models, the persistent unease surrounding certain relationships, the proximity between subject and vulnerability that his work does not attempt to conceal. These are frequently debated, often simplified, and rarely integrated into the structure of the work itself. They should be. For the same reason that the burned drawing matters: they indicate where the system reacts. And reaction, as you will recall, is the clearest evidence of boundary. One might also note, with some administrative interest, the later fate of his work–its confiscation, its dispersal, its implication in cases of Nazi-era looting, and its subsequent recovery through legal processes still unfolding in the present. Even here, the pattern persists. The work does not escape the system. It continues to circulate– through it, across it, and occasionally– against it.

Terminus visus est locus discursūs. (A visible boundary is a site of discourse.)

Students should be encouraged to observe this carefully. To cross a boundary is to end a conversation. To reveal a boundary is to begin one. Schiele, despite appearances, does not destroy the frame. He forces it to appear. And once visible, it becomes increasingly difficult to ignore where it was all along.

Yours in measured proximity and controlled exposure,

B. Judous

9

Dear Mr Jaded Muse,

It is with some hesitation that I turn to Amedeo Modigliani, whose life has been subjected to a degree of romanticisation so persistent that it now functions as a secondary framework through which the work is received. This must be addressed. Modigliani is not significant because he suffered. He is significant because his suffering has been rendered legible. You will note that narratives of addiction, illness, and early death–tuberculosis, alcoholism, narcotics, and the now obligatory tale of the doomed artist in Montparnasse–are consistently positioned as explanatory structures, as though decline were a necessary precondition for artistic production. This is, of course, unsustainable as a general principle.

Dolor non est methodus, sed narratio post factum. (Suffering is not a method, but a narrative after the fact.)

Consider the portraits: elongated necks, mask-like faces, eyes often left blank or asymmetrically defined. These are not symptoms. They are– decisions. Formal, consistent, and remarkably controlled. The stylisation draws as much from African sculpture, Cycladic forms, and Renaissance portraiture as from any supposed interior collapse. The reduction of detail is not fatigue. The distortion is not instability. It is– selection. Students, however, prefer the simpler explanation. They look at the distortion and see biography. They look at the biography and assume necessity. This is inversion. What occurs in Modigliani's case is not the transformation of suffering into art, but the transformation of art into a readable form of suffering. The paintings are not evidence of decline. They are made to appear as such– after the fact. Even his 1917 exhibition in Paris, closed by police due to the explicit display of his nudes in a gallery window, is frequently cited as proof of his transgressive condition. In reality, it demonstrates something far more mundane: the system's sensitivity to display rather than production. The paintings existed. They circulated. They became problematic only when made too visible, too public, too direct. You will recognise the pattern. Students are particularly vulnerable to this mechanism. They begin to aestheticise their own instability, treating exhaustion, uncertainty, and excess as materials rather than conditions. This is inefficient. Instability, when styled, ceases to function. Modigliani's work does not depend on his decline. It is, rather, that his decline has been made to depend on the work in order to sustain its narrative coherence–culminating, as students are so fond of noting, in his death in 1920, followed almost immediately by the suicide of Jeanne Hébuterne, a detail so narratively complete it has been absorbed without resistance. The story stabilises the work. The work does not require the story. The distinction, while subtle, is necessary. We must therefore discourage the belief that difficulty, in itself, produces value. Difficulty produces difficulty. Value emerges elsewhere–through form, consistency, and the capacity of the work to withstand interpretation without collapsing into explanation. There is, however, a further development, which extends this logic beyond the artist's life and into the afterlife of the work itself. Modigliani is now one of the most frequently forged artists in the world. This is not incidental. It is–structural. His works were poorly documented. Drawings were exchanged informally–for meals, for drinks, for temporary stability. Attribution remained unstable. The conditions of production were loose, dispersed, and only partially recorded. The result is not merely uncertainty. It is reproducibility. Forgery, in this context, is not simply criminal activity. It is the continuation of legibility under altered conditions. Consider the repeated scandals: exhibitions filled with counterfeit works, such as the 2017 Genoa seizure; the infamous "Livorno heads" of 1984, in which fabricated sculptures were briefly accepted as authentic; the persistent circulation of fraudulent Modiglianis through markets unable to stabilise authorship. Even experts disagree. Even institutions hesitate. Authenticity, here, becomes not a fixed condition, but a site of negotiation. The work no longer requires the artist to generate meaning. It generates dispute. There are also cases in which his paintings have been implicated in theft, wartime looting, and high-profile legal battles over ownership. A work such as *Seated Man with a Cane* becomes less an image than a contested object–circulating through offshore holdings, legal claims, and restitution cases that extend its significance far beyond its initial production.

Again, nothing unusual. But instructive. For what we observe is this: the narrative of instability attached to the artist now migrates to the work itself. Uncertainty becomes value. Ambiguity becomes market condition. The system does not correct this. It absorbs it. Even the mythology of his life–his so-called "accursed" temperament, his excess, his volatility–becomes part of this extended structure. Stories of violence, of erratic behaviour, of dissolution, whether exaggerated or not, function less as biography than as reinforcement. They stabilise the narrative. They ensure that the work continues to be read through the same lens: suffering made visible. Students should be particularly cautious here. For this is the most dangerous inversion of all: to believe that suffering produces form, rather than recognising that form produces the appearance of suffering.

Forma non ex ruina nascitur; ruina ex forma legitur. (Form does not arise from ruin; ruin is read from form.)

And once this reading is established, it persists. Across exhibitions. Across markets. Across time. Even, and perhaps especially, where certainty fails.

Yours in narrative correction and aesthetic restraint,

B. Judous

10

Dear Mr Jaded Muse,

It has become necessary, though not without some reluctance, to address Marcel Duchamp, whose position within the historical narrative has been so thoroughly absorbed into the language of innovation that it now risks being mistaken for disruption. This is not, I think, accurate. Duchamp does not disrupt the system. He– relocates it. You will observe that his most cited interventions–the so-called *readymades*–are consistently framed as acts of provocation: the selection of ordinary objects, repositioned within an artistic context, presented as though the act of designation were sufficient to constitute transformation. Students, encountering this gesture, tend to experience a brief but intense sense of liberation. This is unfortunate. For what Duchamp demonstrates is not freedom from artistic constraint, but the transfer of constraint from production to selection.

Non fit; eligitur. (It is not made; it is chosen.)

Consider *Fountain* (1917), that most efficient of conceptual irritants: a urinal, inverted, signed, submitted. The object itself is unremarkable. Its form remains unchanged. Its function, temporarily suspended, is not erased. What alters is its position. And with position comes context. And with context comes interpretation. Students often assume that Duchamp removes the necessity of skill. He does not.

He removes the visibility of skill. The labour does not disappear. It is redistributed. From hand to decision. From execution to framing. This distinction is rarely understood at the level required. For the readymade does not eliminate authorship. It– intensifies it. The artist no longer produces the object. The artist produces the condition under which the object may be read. This is a far more demanding operation, though one frequently mistaken for ease. There is, however, a secondary consequence which must not be overlooked. Once the act of selection is established as sufficient, the boundary between art and non-art becomes no longer a fixed division, but a movable threshold. Anything may become art– provided it is correctly positioned. Students, encountering this principle, tend to draw the wrong conclusion. They assume that anything *is* art. This is incorrect. Anything may become art. But only within a system capable of recognising it as such. Recognition is not automatic. It is administered. Duchamp does not abolish the institution. He renders it indispensable. For without the gallery, the exhibition, the discourse, the act of naming and reception, the readymade remains precisely what it was before: unremarkable. It is only when placed within a structure of visibility that it begins to function as art. Thus, the gesture that appears to undermine the institution in fact reveals its necessity. This is not contradiction. It is– clarification. You will also note that Duchamp himself withdraws from production with a degree of deliberation that has been variously interpreted as indifference, strategy, or refusal. He produces infrequently. He plays chess. He allows others to speak on his behalf. This, too, is misread. Withdrawal is not absence. It is– control of appearance. By reducing output, Duchamp increases the interpretive pressure placed upon what remains. Each work carries more weight, not because it contains more, but because it is positioned within a field that expects it to signify. Scarcity becomes amplification. Even authorship itself begins to loosen. Replicas of *Fountain* are produced. Originals become uncertain. The object is less important than the designation. The designation less important than its recognition. We arrive, therefore, at a condition in which authorship is no longer tied to origin, but to circulation. The work exists– where it is acknowledged. Students should find this unsettling. For it removes the final refuge of certainty. If the work is not defined by making and not secured by originality, then it exists only within a system that may accept or refuse it.

Quod nominatur, existit. (That which is named exists.)

This is not liberation. It is– dependency. Duchamp does not free the artist from the system. He makes the artist– inseparable from it.

Yours in delegated authorship and controlled designation,

B. Judous

11

Dear Mr Jaded Muse,

It has been suggested–most often by those with a preference for stylisation over structure–that Aubrey Beardsley represents a form of aesthetic deviance, a deliberate flirtation with the perverse intended to unsettle the sensibilities of his time. This is, I think, only partially accurate. Beardsley does not transgress. He decorates transgression. You will observe that his work, associated with the *fin-de-siècle* and the broader Decadent movement, does not dismantle propriety so much as render it ornamental. Ink becomes incision. Line becomes excess made precise. The grotesque is refined, the erotic abstracted, the unacceptable arranged with such compositional clarity that it invites not rejection, but a kind of aesthetic satisfaction. What appears, at first glance, as violation is, upon closer inspection– arrangement. Consider the illustrations for *Salome* (1894), where biblical narrative is filtered through elongated silhouettes, flattened perspective, and theatrical perversity. The figures do not erupt from the page. They adhere to it. The erotic is present, but stylised. The grotesque is visible, but controlled. The line, so often described as excessive, is in fact disciplined to a degree that borders on administrative precision. Nothing escapes. Everything is contained within design. This presents a complication. You will recall our earlier position that visibility, when mismanaged, accelerates absorption. However, Beardsley demonstrates that certain forms of excess–when sufficiently stylised–are not merely absorbed, but desired.

Vitium ornatum recipitur. (Vice, when adorned, is received.)

This is inconvenient. For if transgression can be made decorative, then its disruptive potential becomes indistinguishable from its aesthetic appeal. What was intended–or later retrospectively described–as destabilising becomes, in practice, circulatory. It does not resist the system. It moves through it. Students are particularly susceptible to this condition. They adopt surface irregularities–distortion, provocation, ambiguity–without recognising that these gestures, when rendered too coherent, cease to function as disturbance. They become–style. And style, as we have not yet formally admitted, is one of the system's most efficient mechanisms of containment. It does not suppress deviation. It formats it. Once formatted, deviation becomes recognisable. Once recognisable, it becomes repeatable. Once repeatable, it becomes safe. This is the precise point at which transgression ceases to operate as such. Beardsley's line, so often described as radical, achieves a level of clarity that ensures its reception. The viewer is not excluded. They are invited. Even where discomfort persists, it is structured. The eye moves smoothly. The composition resolves. The image, however strange its content, remains aesthetically complete. This is not rupture. It is– completion under altered terms. There is, however, a secondary difficulty. Beardsley's work emerges within a cultural moment already predisposed toward aesthetic excess. The Decadent movement does not resist ornament. It requires it. Thus, what appears as deviation may already be aligned with expectation. The perverse is not introduced into the system. It is– refined within it. Even his association with scandal–his involvement with *The Yellow Book*, his proximity to the aesthetic controversies surrounding Oscar Wilde–does not destabilise his position so much as intensify it. He is dismissed, reabsorbed, circulated. Illness, too–his tuberculosis, his awareness of limited time–enters the narrative not as disruption, but as amplification. The work becomes more intricate, more excessive, more controlled. Nothing loosens. Everything– tightens. Students, observing this, often assume that extremity produces significance. They are mistaken. Extremity, when disciplined, produces ornament. And ornament, once stabilised, produces style. We must therefore consider a possibility that remains,

I think, insufficiently examined, that what we have been describing as resistance is, in certain instances, simply a more elaborate form of agreement. Not conscious, perhaps. But– structural. Beardsley does not dismantle the system. He demonstrates how far it can extend without appearing to do so. He shows us that the unacceptable, when sufficiently arranged, ceases to threaten. It– pleases. *Ornamentum an error?*

Non liquet. (Ornament or error? It is not clear.)

And it is precisely this uncertainty, Mr Muse, that should give us pause. For a system that can aestheticise its own transgressions no longer requires correction. It requires only refinement.

Yours in decorative deviation and interpretive hesitation,

B. Judous

P.S.

Limes visus mutatur. (A seen boundary shifts.) And once shifted, it reasserts itself elsewhere.

12

Dear Mr Jaded Muse,

We must now turn to Banksy, whose continued presence within the system presents a peculiar challenge to the principles we have thus far maintained. Banksy is frequently described as anonymous. This is inaccurate. He is not anonymous. He is– circulated as anonymous. You will observe that anonymity, in this instance, does not reduce visibility but intensifies it. The absence of a stable authorial identity becomes not a limitation, but a mechanism of distribution. The work travels not despite the obscured origin, but because of it. The absence itself becomes the signature.

Absentia auctoris praesentiam auget. (The absence of the author increases presence.)

This presents a complication. We have previously suggested that visibility leads to absorption, and that legibility must be carefully regulated. Yet here, the removal of the author appears to produce a form of hyper-legibility–an intensified clarity of gesture, stripped of biographical interference, and therefore more easily consumed at scale. The image arrives without friction. It does not require explanation. It– circulates. Consider *Girl with Balloon* or *Flower Thrower*: images so immediately legible that their origin becomes almost irrelevant to their function. They operate not as objects, but as signals–compressed, repeatable, and infinitely transferable across surfaces, platforms, and contexts. Even interventions such as the partial shredding of *Girl with Balloon* at auction do not interrupt the work's circulation. They– reassign it. Destruction becomes event. Event becomes image. Image becomes– further circulation. The work does not end. It multiplies. Students, encountering this, often conclude that authorship is unnecessary. They imagine that by obscuring themselves–through anonymity, collectivity, or conceptual withdrawal–they may achieve a similar effect. This is rarely successful. For Banksy's anonymity is not absence. It is– structure. It is maintained, reproduced, and–one suspects–selectively reinforced by the very systems it appears to critique: galleries, auction houses, media cycles, and the continuous demand for legible dissent. Anonymity, in this case, is not opposition to visibility. It is– a refinement of it. There is also the matter of authenticity, which in this instance becomes increasingly unstable. Works appear, disappear, are authenticated, contested, reproduced, misattributed. Entire mechanisms emerge–certification bodies, verification processes, institutional endorsements–designed not to stabilise authorship, but to manage its instability. The proliferation of forgeries and disputed works does not diminish engagement. It– intensifies it. The system does not reject uncertainty. It monetises it. Authenticity, therefore, ceases to function as a fixed property of the work. It becomes a temporary agreement.

An agreement between circulation and belief. This is, as you will appreciate, inconvenient. For if authenticity is distributed, then it can no longer serve as a stable ground for value. And if authorship is obscured, then critique itself begins to resemble branding. You will also note that Banksy's work frequently positions itself as oppositional: anti-capitalist, anti-institutional, resistant to authority. Yet this resistance is consistently legible, repeatable, and–most importantly–collectable. It does not evade the system. It feeds it. The image critiques commodification while being commodified. The gesture resists authority while increasing its own recognisability. This is not contradiction. It is–compatibility at scale. Students must be particularly cautious here. For anonymity, when misunderstood, appears as freedom. It is not. Freedom withdraws. Banksy does not withdraw. He– distributes. And in distribution, he achieves something far more difficult than disappearance: he becomes unfixed, yet unmistakable.

Quod diffunditur, mutatur. (That which is distributed is altered.)

I will not pursue this further at present. Though one suspects, Mr Muse, that we are approaching a condition in which the artist is no longer required to be present at all– only– recognisable.

Yours in structured absence and circulating identity,

B. Judous

13

Dear Mr Jaded Muse,

It is with a degree of administrative caution that I approach Damien Hirst, whose work appears, at first glance, to confirm several of our earlier positions regarding visibility, shock, and system absorption. On closer inspection, however, a complication emerges. Hirst does not test the system. He anticipates it. You will observe that his work–whether involving preserved animals in vitrines, serialised spot paintings, or controlled displays of material excess such as *For the Love of God*, the diamond-encrusted skull–arrives already framed. The conditions of interpretation are not discovered after presentation, but embedded within the work's initial conditions of reception. The work does not generate discourse. It– pre-allocates it. Shock is present. But it does not unfold. It arrives complete.

Effectus ante causam disponitur. (The effect is arranged before the cause.)

This produces a curious effect. The shock is immediate, but short-lived. The work stabilises rapidly, not because it resolves itself, but because its resolution has already been distributed across the system that receives it: galleries, auction houses, press commentary, and the predictable sequence of outrage followed by valuation. Reaction becomes– procedure. Students often misinterpret this as confidence. They assume that clarity of intention produces strength of work. This is, in most cases, premature. Clarity,

when introduced too early, reduces the operational space in which uncertainty might otherwise function as a generative force. The work becomes legible before it has had the opportunity to resist its own interpretation. Hirst avoids this constraint– but not by preserving ambiguity within the object. Instead, he– relocates uncertainty. The instability is not within the work. It is– around it. In questions of fabrication, delegation, authorship, production systems, and the increasingly industrial logic of contemporary art-making. The studio becomes indistinguishable from the factory; the gesture becomes indistinguishable from the commission. Assistants execute. Systems replicate. The artist designates. This is not a disappearance of authorship. It is– its expansion. Authorship no longer resides in the hand. It resides in the orchestration of conditions under which the work appears.
The object, therefore, becomes stable. Repeatable. Predictable. It is the system that absorbs the instability. Value fluctuates. Authenticity is negotiated. Intent becomes retrospective. The work remains unchanged. This inversion is not merely notable. It is– structural. For it suggests that instability need not reside within the work at all. It may instead be displaced into the infrastructure of its production and reception, where meaning is continuously recalibrated without requiring alteration of the object itself.
We are no longer dealing with unstable works. We are dealing with stable works within unstable systems. This marks, I think, a significant adjustment to our earlier assumptions. We have previously maintained that the work must preserve a degree of internal tension–of incompletion, ambiguity, or withheld resolution–in order to remain productive. Hirst proposes an alternative: that the work may be fully resolved, provided the system

around it is not. Students will find this tempting. It should be resisted. For the ability to displace instability outward depends upon a level of structural control rarely available to those still operating within the conditions of instruction. Without such control, clarity collapses into closure. Closure produces silence. And silence, as we have established, is indistinguishable from disappearance. There is, however, a final concern. If the system is now capable of generating and sustaining instability independently of the work– if value, authorship, and interpretation can circulate without requiring internal resistance– then the function of the artist becomes increasingly uncertain. Not absent. But– optional in ways that were previously inconceivable. I am not yet prepared to formalise this. Though I note, with some unease, that the system appears increasingly comfortable operating without our permission.

Ubi instabilitas residet? Quaestio manet. (Where does instability reside? The question remains.)

And one suspects, Mr Muse, that the answer–when it arrives–may no longer require us to recognise it.

Yours in pre-emptive coherence and displaced uncertainty,

B. Judous

14

Dear Mr Jaded Muse,

It has been proposed–most often with a tone of cautious sincerity–that Tracey Emin represents a form of radical exposure, a direct presentation of the self unmediated by aesthetic convention. This is an attractive reading. It is also, I suspect, incomplete. Emin does not expose the self. She exposes the conditions under which exposure is recognised. You will observe that works such as *My Bed* (1998), often cited as the paradigmatic instance of autobiographical immediacy, do not simply present material. They– stage it. The bed is not merely unmade; it is positioned. The surrounding detritus–bottles, sheets, fragments of bodily and emotional exhaustion–is not accidental residue, but selected index. Each element is retained, arranged, and framed in such a way that it becomes legible as evidence. The work does not present life. It presents the recognisable structure of aftermath. One might even note, with some precision, that the work is frequently described–by both artist and audience–as resembling a "crime scene." This is not metaphorical excess. It is– instruction. A crime scene is not the event itself. It is the arrangement through which the event becomes readable. Similarly, works such as *Everyone I Have Ever Slept With 1963-1995* do not function as confession in any unstructured sense. They are catalogues, enumerations, systems of naming intimacy into legibility.

Even her neon tcxts those brief declarations of longing, regret, or assertion–operate as compressed, circulatable forms of interiority. The self is not revealed. It is–formatted.

Expositio sine structura non legitur. (Exposure without structure is not read.)

Students, encountering this, often conclude that honesty is sufficient. They bring forward fragments of lived experience, assuming that proximity to the self guarantees significance. This is rarely the case. The system does not respond to exposure. It responds to– recognisable forms of exposure. Unstructured vulnerability does not circulate. It remains– private. Only when organised–framed, edited, positioned–does it become visible within the system at all. There is, however, a complication. We have previously suggested that visibility accelerates absorption, that what is shown becomes contained. Yet Emin's work appears, at least initially, to resist immediate stabilisation–not because it withholds, but because it presents in excess of expectation. It offers vulnerability in a form already culturally legible. Confession. Autobiography. Emotional disclosure. Arranged as object. This is, as you will note, dangerously close to what we earlier described as mismanaged visibility. And yet– it functions. One might therefore consider whether exposure, when sufficiently structured, ceases to be exposure at all. Whether what we call "self" in these contexts is not the origin of the work, but its most efficient organisational principle. The work does not emerge from the self. The self is assembled for the work. There are, of course, biographical elements that resist easy incorporation into aesthetic discourse–experiences of trauma, of sexual violence, of personal crisis, which Emin has neither concealed nor simplified.

Students tend to approach these with a degree of moral certainty that is, while understandable, analytically unproductive. For the question is not whether these experiences are real. They are. The question is: how they become visible? Once articulated within the work, they enter a system that does not distinguish between sincerity and structure. It receives, interprets, circulates, and–inevitably–assigns value. Even forgery participates in this condition. The imitation of Emin's work–its reproduction by others, its circulation under false attribution–does not undermine its logic. It confirms it. For if the self can be structured, it can be replicated. Students should find this deeply unsettling. For it suggests that what appears most personal may, under certain conditions, become transferable.

An revelatio sit constructio? Fortasse. (Is revelation a construction? Perhaps.)

I hesitate to formalise this. Though one suspects, Mr Muse, that we are approaching a point at which the distinction between expression and arrangement becomes increasingly difficult to maintain– particularly for those who continue to believe they are the origin of what they present.

Yours in arranged vulnerability and selective disclosure,

B. Judous

15

Dear Mr Jaded Muse,

We must now consider Ai Weiwei, whose work is frequently described in terms of political intervention, as though its primary function were to oppose rather than to reorganise. This is, I think, a misalignment of emphasis. Ai Weiwei does not destroy objects. He– redistributes their meaning. You will observe that the act–whether the staged dropping of a Han dynasty urn, the vast installation of *Sunflower Seeds*, or the systematic documentation of surveillance and detention–does not result in absence. The object persists. Though altered. Its significance is not erased, but displaced into circulation: photographic, institutional, archival. Even the most decisive gesture–destruction itself–is preserved. Not as an event, but as– image.

Destructio est translatio. (Destruction is translation.)

Students, encountering this, often assume that negation produces critique. They dismantle, remove, or refuse, believing that absence itself constitutes a position. This is rarely sustainable. Absence, unless structured, produces silence. Silence, unless framed, produces indifference. Ai Weiwei avoids this outcome with precision. Every gesture of negation is immediately reabsorbed into visibility: recorded, distributed, exhibited, debated. The act does not disappear. It– multiplies. Destruction becomes documentation. Documentation becomes discourse. Discourse becomes– circulation. Which raises a difficulty. If destruction must be seen in order to function, then it is no longer purely destructive. It becomes dependent. Dependent upon the very systems of visibility it appears to oppose. We have, I believe, encountered this condition before. Though it now appears more explicit. There is also a secondary complication. The more the gesture circulates, the more stable its meaning becomes. What begins as interruption resolves into recognisable form–political artwork, activist intervention, institutional critique–each category reinforcing the system's capacity to absorb dissent without requiring structural alteration. Resistance, in such conditions, does not exit the system. It– clarifies it.

Quod resistit, etiam innititur. (That which resists also relies.)

You will also note that the system, when confronted directly, responds not by collapsing, but by reasserting its own mechanisms. Ai Weiwei's detention in 2011–officially framed as a matter of tax evasion, though widely understood as a response to his criticism of state authority –does not remove him from circulation. It– intensifies it. Eighty-one days of detention became: international attention, institutional advocacy, renewed visibility. The attempt at suppression becomes another form of distribution. Interrogation produces narrative. Restriction produces documentation. Even the conditions of confinement are translated into material: testimony, image, reconstruction. The system does not silence. It generates further content. This is not failure. It is– function. Students must be particularly cautious here. For they are often tempted to believe that opposition exists outside the system it addresses. This is rarely the case. Opposition requires visibility. Visibility requires structure. Structure requires recognition. And recognition, as we have observed, is never neutral. Ai Weiwei does not escape the system. He operates within it– at a point of maximum tension. He does not remove meaning. He– reassigns it. From object, to act, to record, to circulation. The work is no longer what remains. It is– what continues to move. There is, however, a final difficulty. If destruction must be preserved, if resistance must be visible, if critique must circulate– then the distinction between opposition and participation becomes increasingly difficult to maintain. I do not propose to resolve this. Though one suspects, Mr Muse, that the system has already accounted for such distinctions– and found them, if not irrelevant, then at least manageable.

Yours in visible negation and redistributed form,

B. Judous

16

Dear Mr Jaded Muse,

It is with a degree of caution that I address Maurizio Cattelan, whose work presents a particular difficulty for any system that relies upon the distinction between seriousness and its absence. Cattelan does not critique. He displaces. You will observe that his gestures–whether a banana duct-taped to a wall (*Comedian*), a functioning gold toilet (*America*), or earlier acts of institutional satire and sculptural misdirection–do not operate by opposing the system, but by revealing its capacity to accommodate almost anything, including its own parody. This is not resistance. It is– elastic exposure. The system does not break. It– bends. And in bending, it reveals not its weakness, but its range.

Systema ridendo se extendit. (The system extends itself through laughter.)

Students, encountering this, often assume that humour destabilises authority. They produce work that gestures toward irony, absurdity, or refusal, believing that these modes exist outside conventional structures of meaning. This is– optimistic. For humour, when recognised, is immediately contained. It becomes commentary. Commentary becomes position. Position becomes category. The joke settles into discourse like any other material. Laughter does not suspend the system. It– confirms it. Cattelan appears to understand this with precision. His work does not preserve humour as rupture. It allows humour to– collapse into seriousness, and seriousness to– re-emerge as humour. This oscillation is not incidental. It is – structural. You will observe that *Comedian*, however trivial its initial gesture appears, rapidly becomes: debate, valuation, institutional framing, and eventual canonisation. The joke does not resist interpretation. It– accelerates it. Similarly, *America*, installed as a functioning gold toilet within a museum, invites both use and reflection. It is absurd, excessive, materially explicit–and yet entirely legible within the structures it appears to mock. Visitors participate. Institutions endorse. Meaning circulates. Nothing escapes. Even scandal, where it appears, functions less as disruption than as a form of circulation management. The work attracts attention, generates discourse, and stabilises into recognisable significance with remarkable efficiency. The system does not reject the joke. It– processes it. This is, I should note, structurally consistent with our earlier observations. Though here, the instability is not located in meaning, nor in visibility, but in tone. Tone becomes the variable through which the work resists fixation. Not by withholding, but by– shifting. A work may be read as humorous, then serious, then ironic, then critical, without ever settling into a single interpretive position. This does not prevent interpretation. It proliferates it. Students, however, tend to misapply this principle. They attempt humour as strategy, irony as defence, absurdity as position. But without structural awareness, humour collapses into novelty. Novelty into distraction. Distraction into– irrelevance. Cattelan's work avoids this outcome not because it is inherently more absurd, but because it is precisely calibrated to remain legible at every stage of its transformation. The joke is never lost. It is– reassigned.

Gravitas et levitas convertuntur. (Gravity and lightness convert into each other.)

And it is this conversion, Mr Muse, that now presents the greater difficulty. For if seriousness can become humour, and humour can become seriousness, then tone itself ceases to function as a stable indicator of meaning. One is no longer able to determine whether the work is to be taken seriously– or whether that distinction has already been absorbed into its operation. I find myself, increasingly, unable to identify the point at which interpretation begins. Which suggests– with some reluctance– that conversion itself may now be the dominant system function. And that what we have been calling meaning is, perhaps, only the residue of its movement.

Yours in displaced seriousness and tonal uncertainty,

B. Judous

17

Dear Mr Jaded Muse,

It has become necessary to address Andres Serrano, whose work is frequently misread as an attack upon sanctity, when in fact it operates as a controlled activation of it. The most cited example, *Piss Christ* (1987), is typically described in terms of blasphemy. This is– imprecise. Serrano does not desecrate sacred objects. He re-stages sanctity under altered material conditions. You will observe that the image, a crucifix submerged in fluid presented as bodily waste, does not eliminate religious significance. On the contrary, it intensifies it. The sacred does not disappear under insult; it becomes newly visible. Visible not as belief, but as category under pressure.

Sacrum non tollitur; reconfiguratur. (The sacred is not removed; it is reconfigured.)

Students frequently misunderstand this mechanism. They assume that offence is a form of negation, that to provoke is to dismantle belief. This is not supported by evidence. Offence, when successfully registered, does not erase meaning. It– activates it. You will observe the sequence: outrage, reproduction, institutional response, funding controversy, media amplification. Each stage does not diminish the work. It– extends it. The image does not exist in isolation. It exists within the network of reactions it produces. Meaning is not destroyed. It is distributed. The system does not reject sacrilege. It– organises it. This is not contradiction. It is– operation. There is, however, a more subtle observation. Serrano's work reveals that sacredness is not a fixed property of objects, but a relational intensity triggered by context, framing, and reaction. The crucifix, removed from controversy, is an image. Placed within provocation, it becomes– event. Event produces discourse. Discourse produces– structure. And structure stabilises what initially appeared unstable.

The same image, removed from its discursive environment, loses its volatility almost immediately. Which suggests– with some precision– that sanctity does not reside in the object at all. It resides in the response. Students should find this troubling. For it implies that the sacred is not protected from violation. It is produced by it. The more intense the reaction, the more clearly the category of the sacred is defined. Which raises an uncomfortable possibility. That the sacred and the scandalous may not be opposites at all. But– reflections. Structurally identical phenomena, differentiated only by the direction and intensity of attention. Reverence stabilises. Outrage accelerates. Both– sustain.

Profanum et sacrum in eadem machina. (The profane and the sacred operate within the same mechanism.)

I hesitate to pursue this further. Though one begins to suspect, Mr Muse, that what we have been calling belief may be less a property of objects, and more a function of the system's ability to organise response around them.

Yours in managed outrage and redistributed reverence,

B. Judous

18

Dear Mr Jaded Muse,

We must now address Richard Prince, whose practice presents a difficulty not of production, but of possession. Prince does not make images. He– relocates them. You will observe that his work–whether the Instagram portraits, the *New Portraits* series, or earlier appropriations of Marlboro advertising imagery–does not transform its material in any immediately visible sense. The image remains recognisable. Intact. And troublingly familiar. The cowboy still rides. The smile still performs. The photograph still belongs–at least in appearance–to its original source. What changes is not the object. It is– its position. More precisely, its position within the system of attribution.

Mutatio loci mutat rem. (Change of place changes the thing.)

This, at first glance, appears minimal. It is not. For relocation, when recognised, produces a shift not in form, but in authority. The image ceases to function as evidence of its origin and begins to function as evidence of its reassignment. It is no longer *from* somewhere. It is now– *of* somewhere else. Students, encountering this, often conclude that originality is unnecessary. They assume that by recontextualising existing material, they may inherit its significance. This is rarely successful. For recontextualisation is not an act. It is– a condition. A condition that must be recognised by the system in order to function. Prince's work operates not because the gesture is performed, but because it is *accepted*. Galleries exhibit it. Courts debate it. Collectors acquire it. Audiences circulate it. Without this recognition, the gesture collapses into repetition without difference– duplication without consequence. Which is to say: nothing happens. There is, however, a more precise difficulty. If meaning is produced by relocation, then authorship becomes unstable. The origin of the image no longer guarantees its interpretation. Nor its value. Nor even its identity. The author becomes secondary to the act of recognition that reassigns the work its position. One might say, though I do so with some reluctance, that authorship has shifted from creation to designation. This is... administratively efficient. And conceptually inconvenient. For if authorship is no longer origin but assignment, then it ceases to belong to the maker at all. It becomes a function of the system. Allocated. Confirmed. Circulated. Students tend to find this liberating. They should not. For liberation, in this case, is indistinguishable from dependency. If authorship must be recognised in order to exist, then it is no longer self-generated. It is granted. And what is granted can be withheld. There is also a secondary instability. Prince's work suggests that the image itself is no longer the primary site of artistic activity. The work occurs elsewhere: in framing, in positioning, in the subtle but decisive shift that converts the already-visible into the newly legible. The image is not made. It is– activated. Which raises an increasingly difficult question. If the work is not located in the object and not entirely in the maker, then where, precisely, does it reside? In the act of selection? In the context of display? In the moment of recognition? Or– more troublingly– in the system's ability to stabilise all three at once? I find that the distinction between making and assigning is becoming increasingly administrative. And administration, as you will appreciate, is rarely a source of clarity. It produces structure. It produces order. It produces authority. But it does not, as a rule, explain itself.

Quis auctor? Incertum est. (Who is the author? It is uncertain.)

Though I begin to suspect, Mr Muse, that the question may already be incorrectly framed. For if authorship can be reassigned, then perhaps it was never located where we first believed it to be.

Yours in displaced authorship and circulating form,

B. Judous

19

Dear Mr Jaded Muse,

It has become necessary–though not entirely comfortable–to address the matter of scandal within the art world, particularly in its more elaborate manifestations: forgery, misattribution, and the sustained misrecognition of authenticity. You will be aware of the various incidents to which I refer. Paintings attributed to the wrong hand, most notably those associated with Wolfgang Beltracchi. Works authenticated through confidence rather than verification. Entire collections constructed upon consensus rather than material certainty. These are not, as is often suggested, failures of the system. They are expressions of it.

Fides facit veritatem. (Belief makes truth.)

You will observe that a forged work, when accepted, does not function differently from an authentic one. It circulates. It accumulates value. It attracts interpretation. It is discussed, exhibited, insured, and admired with appropriate seriousness. Its aesthetic life is indistinguishable. The eye does not protest. The discourse does not falter. The market does not hesitate. Everything proceeds– as expected. Its status as forgery becomes relevant only when exposed. And even then, its significance rarely diminishes. It merely changes category. From artwork to case study. From object to narrative. From possession to lesson. The system does not discard it. It reclassifies it. Students, encountering this, often experience a brief but intense destabilisation. They begin to question the foundations of artistic value, the authority of expertise, and the reliability of institutional validation. This is... productive. But short-lived. For the system absorbs scandal with remarkable efficiency. What appears to threaten its stability instead becomes part of its internal documentation. The forgery becomes discourse. The deception becomes curriculum. The error becomes–history. And history, as you will have noticed, is one of the system's most effective stabilising devices. There is, however, a more troubling implication. If belief sustains value, and value sustains circulation, then authenticity is no longer a fixed property of the work. It becomes–conditional. Operational. Activated when required, and quietly suspended when inconvenient. Which is to say: authenticity does not determine value. Value determines authenticity. This inversion is rarely acknowledged directly. It is simply maintained. You will note that the moment of exposure does not erase what came before. The work has already circulated. Already been seen. Already been written about. Already believed. Exposure does not undo this. It reorganises it. The narrative shifts. The object remains. The system adjusts. One might therefore conclude –though I do so with some hesitation–that the distinction between authentic and inauthentic is not foundational, but administrative. A classification applied– after the fact. And revised– as needed. I find myself increasingly uncertain whether the system is concerned with truth at all. Or whether it is simply concerned with maintaining the conditions under which belief can continue to operate without interruption.

Verum et falsum cohabitant. (Truth and falsehood dwell together.)

Though I begin to suspect, Mr Muse, that they do not merely coexist. They– depend upon one another. For without the possibility of error, belief would have nothing to stabilise itself against. And without belief– there would be no value to protect.

Yours in sustained ambiguity and institutional belief,

B. Judous

20

Dear Mr Jaded Muse,

Forgery, as it is most commonly understood, is treated as a violation–an intrusion upon authenticity, a disruption of trust, a failure of verification. This is, I think, a reassuring misinterpretation. Forgery does not undermine authority. It reveals how little of it is required. You will observe that this is nowhere more evident than in the case of the so-called *Salvator Mundi*, attributed to Leonardo da Vinci and subject to prolonged institutional dispute, fluctuating attribution, and ultimately a record-breaking auction sale of approximately $450 million. What is significant here is not whether the painting is "truly" by Leonardo, or by workshop hands, or by later intervention. It is that the question itself becomes structurally productive. Uncertainty, in this case, does not diminish value. It generates it.

Auctoritas non invenitur; constituitur. (Authority is not discovered; it is constituted.)

You will observe that a convincing attribution does not succeed through certainty alone. Certainty, in fact, is often insufficient. It succeeds because it is received within a framework of institutional belief: curators, experts, provenance records, conservation analysis, market timing, and the narrative coherence required for high-value circulation. Each element does not confirm the work independently. They– align. And alignment, when sufficiently reinforced, produces the appearance of inevitability. In short, the system cooperates.

Systema falsum suscipit si bene formatum est. (The system accepts the false if it is well-formed.)

Students, encountering this, often experience a brief enthusiasm for subversion. They imagine that by destabilising authorship, or exposing uncertainty in attribution, they might weaken institutional authority itself. This is– optimistic. For the exposure of fragility does not diminish the system. It– refines it. Doubt becomes documentation. Disagreement becomes discourse. Dispute becomes– visibility. And visibility, as we have repeatedly observed, is rarely destructive. It is– generative. The contested object does not lose status. It acquires layers. Interpretation accumulates. Narrative thickens. Value– intensifies. There is, however, a complication that is less easily absorbed. If authority can be convincingly produced through alignment of narrative, expertise, and circulation, then its origin becomes secondary. Or perhaps– irrelevant. The distinction between authentic and constructed shifts from essential to procedural. It is no longer a question of *what is true*, but of *what can be sustained as true* within the system's operational limits. Which raises an uncomfortable possibility: That authority is not possessed. It is performed. Maintained through repetition, through agreement, through the continuous reinforcement of its own conditions. And like all performances, it requires an audience. I note, in passing, that this implication may extend beyond art objects. I will not elaborate. Though I am beginning to notice how often that restraint is required.

Auctoritas agitur, non datur. (Authority is performed, not given.)

And I find myself wondering, Mr Muse, whether what we have been calling "truth" is not the foundation of authority but its most convincing effect.

Yours in constructed legitimacy and procedural truth,

B. Judous

21

Dear Mr Jaded Muse,

We must now consider the market–not as an external force acting upon art, but as a condition through which art becomes legible at all. It is a common error, particularly among students, to imagine that value is assigned after the fact–that the work exists, and the market responds. This is... comforting. It is also incorrect. The market does not follow the work. It calibrates it.

Valor non sequitur; constituitur. (Value does not follow; it is constituted.)

You will observe that works of identical material composition may occupy radically different positions within the system. One circulates through institutions, auctions, publications, collections. It accumulates significance. It acquires language. It becomes visible. Until, eventually, it appears self-evidently important. Another remains inert. Not because it lacks content. Not because it lacks intention. But because it has not been activated by the necessary structures of recognition. The difference is not in the object. It is– in its placement within circulation. More precisely, in its ability to be sustained within circulation. Students, encountering this, often oscillate between resentment and fascination. They suspect–correctly–that value is not entirely correlated with quality, yet they continue to pursue it as though it were. This is productive. For the pursuit of value generates activity. And activity sustains the system that produces value as its observable effect. They work. They submit. They exhibit. They circulate. And in doing so, they reinforce the very structure they believe they are attempting to enter. There is, however, a more delicate observation to be made. If value is calibrated externally–through reception, validation, discourse, and exchange– then the internal state of the work (its intention, coherence, necessity) becomes increasingly difficult to distinguish from its subsequent interpretation. Which is to say: the work is not merely evaluated. It is completed. Completed not in the studio, but in the network that surrounds it. Valuation. Attribution. Institutional framing. Historical placement. Each adds something the work itself does not contain. Each stabilises what would otherwise remain indeterminate. This introduces a difficulty. For we have previously maintained that unfinishedness is a condition to be preserved within the work itself. Yet here, completion appears to occur outside it. Not as resolution, but as– assignment. The work remains unstable. The system stabilises it. I am aware that this creates a contradiction. I am, at present, content to allow it. In fact, I am no longer certain contradiction is the correct description. It may be that what we are observing is not opposition, but distribution. Unfinishedness does not disappear. It relocates. From object to system.

Perfectio extra opus residet. (Completion resides outside the work.)

And if that is so, then the work may not be the primary unit under consideration at all. It may instead be– a node. A temporary point of concentration within a larger field of circulation, where meaning, value, and recognition gather briefly, before moving on. I do not yet know what replaces it. Though I begin to suspect, Mr Muse, that we have been attributing far too much autonomy to the object.

Yours in calibrated value and external completion,

22

Dear Mr Jaded Muse,

It has become increasingly difficult to maintain a stable position on the matter of attribution. You will recall– though I begin to suspect that recall is itself an unreliable mechanism–that we once treated authorship as a structuring principle: a means of locating intention, responsibility, and coherence within the work. This now appears... insufficient. Attribution, as it currently functions, does not describe origin. It– assigns it.

Origo tribuitur, non invenitur. (Origin is assigned, not found.)

You will observe that the same work, when attributed differently, produces not merely alternative readings, but entirely different conditions of legibility. The shift in authorship does not simply reframe the work. It– reconstructs it. A painting attributed to a master is not the same painting attributed to a follower. Not because the material changes– but because the system reorganises itself around it. Value adjusts. Interpretation realigns. Visibility intensifies or recedes. The object remains. The work does not. This is not metaphorical. It is operational. We have already seen this in contested attributions, in works circulating between workshop, master, and follower; in forgeries whose status alters retrospectively without any material change; and in cases where institutional agreement alone determines the coherence of authorship.

The pattern is consistent. Authorship is not discovered. It is applied. And once applied, it behaves as though it had always been there. Students, encountering this, often respond with a form of conceptual fatigue. They begin to suspect that meaning is less stable than they had hoped, and more dependent on context than they can comfortably manage. This is accurate. But not in the way they imagine. For if attribution constructs meaning rather than records it, then the author becomes less a source and more a function. A stabilising node through which interpretation is organised. A point of convergence for discourse, value, and recognition. Not the origin of the work, but the condition under which the work becomes legible. This is not entirely consistent with our earlier reliance on authorial instability. Or rather, it is its continuation. Instability has not been removed. It has been formalised. The author no longer collapses unpredictably. They are introduced precisely where required to stabilise what would otherwise remain indeterminate. I find that both positions can be maintained simultaneously, provided one does not insist upon resolving them. There is, however, a further observation. One that I hesitate to formalise, though it presents itself with increasing clarity. If the author is a function, then it is not necessary that they exist prior to their deployment. They may be constructed retrospectively. Assigned provisionally. Or distributed across multiple positions without requiring consolidation. In such cases, authorship does not precede the work. It follows it. Or perhaps more accurately: it accompanies it, appearing wherever stability is required, and withdrawing when it is not. I note, with some unease, how little resistance this now produces. And how easily the absence of origin is replaced by the performance of it.

Auctor functio est. (The author is a function.)

Though I begin to suspect, Mr Muse, that even this formulation may be unnecessarily restrictive. For a function, at least, implies a degree of consistency. And I am no longer entirely convinced that consistency is being maintained.

Yours in assigned origin and functional identity,

B. Judous

23

Dear Mr Jaded Muse,

It has not escaped my attention–though I cannot be entirely certain when this awareness first stabilised–that certain patterns within our discussions have begun to repeat. This is not, in itself, remarkable. Repetition, as you know, is one of the system's most efficient stabilising mechanisms. A principle, once introduced, does not disappear. It– reappears. Under slightly altered conditions, with adjusted vocabulary, and a degree of tonal variation sufficient to produce the impression of movement. What appears as development is, more often, reoccupation.

Repetitio stabilitatem simulat. (Repetition simulates stability.)

You will observe that many of the positions we have advanced–regarding authorship, attribution, visibility, value, and instability–have returned, though not always in recognisable form. They shift. They rephrase themselves. They redistribute emphasis. And in doing so, they present themselves as though newly derived, when in fact they are structurally continuous. This is... familiar. Students experience a comparable condition. They believe they are progressing through conceptual stages, moving from uncertainty to clarity, from confusion to articulation. When in fact they are– circling. The same structural problems, encountered repeatedly, under increasingly refined descriptions. Each iteration feels like advancement. Each return feels like discovery. We have encouraged this. Or perhaps– we have merely described it accurately enough for it to continue. The distinction, I find, is increasingly difficult to maintain. There is, however, a further complication. If repetition produces the appearance of coherence, then coherence itself may not be a property of the system at all. It may instead be– an effect. A byproduct of recurrence. Generated by the system's need to remain intelligible to itself over time. In other words, the system does not stabilise because it is coherent.

It appears coherent– because it repeats. This introduces a difficulty. For if progression cannot be clearly distinguished from return, then development becomes ambiguous. And ambiguity, while previously useful, now appears to function less as a productive condition and more as a structural inevitability. Which raises a question I hesitate to fully articulate: Are we advancing a framework... or merely participating in its continuation? I note this without resolution. Not because resolution is unavailable, but because it appears unnecessary. Indeed, one begins to suspect that resolution itself may simply be another form of repetition– a familiar gesture of closure, applied at the moment when continuation becomes too visible to ignore.

Circulus an progressus? Incertum manet. (Circle or progress? It remains uncertain.)

And I find myself uncertain whether that uncertainty is genuine, or simply another return of a position I have already occupied– and failed to recognise.

Yours in recurring clarity and structural return,

B. Judous

24

Dear Mr Jaded Muse,

We have, throughout these letters, operated under the assumption–sometimes stated, more often implied–that instruction is occurring. That something is being transmitted. That a position of knowledge is being extended toward a position of reception. That you, as recipient, are positioned to apply, interpret, or at the very least misapply what has been outlined. This assumption now appears... less stable. You will observe that the content of our correspondence does not resolve into actionable guidance. Each principle introduced is subsequently complicated, revised, or quietly undermined by its own extension. A position is established– and then displaced. A framework is proposed– and then redistributed. Clarity appears– briefly– only to be reabsorbed into a wider field of uncertainty. This is not an error. Or if it is, it is a persistent one.

Directio datur ut amittatur. (Direction is given in order to be lost.)

Students, when confronted with such conditions, often respond by seeking clarity elsewhere. They look for stable frameworks, definitive criteria, authoritative conclusions– structures that might anchor interpretation. These are, of course, unavailable. Not because they do not exist, but because their stabilisation would interrupt the very process being described. For if clarity were achieved, movement would cease. And cessation, as we have repeatedly observed, is indistinguishable from conclusion. There is, however, a more disquieting observation. If instruction consistently fails to stabilise understanding, then its function may not be to guide at all. It may instead be– to sustain movement. To maintain a controlled state of interpretive displacement in which certainty is perpetually approached, but never secured. Instruction, in this sense, does not resolve confusion. It– organises it. Structures it. Distributes it across time, across language, across the repeated attempt to arrive at something that remains– just beyond consolidation. It ensures that the subject–if we may still use that term–remains in a condition of productive misalignment: close enough to meaning to continue, but never settled enough to conclude. This condition, I should note, is not accidental. It is– maintained. And it applies equally to the recipient of these letters. Whether that recipient is you– a distinct individual positioned at the end of this correspondence– or whether "you" is simply the name given to a structural position within the system of address, occupied temporarily, and replaceable without consequence– I leave unresolved. Though the distinction, I find, is becoming increasingly difficult to sustain.

Qui docetur movetur. (He who is taught is moved.)

And I begin to suspect, Mr Muse, that movement was never optional– but required. Not as a consequence of instruction, but as its condition.

Yours in directional ambiguity and sustained misalignment,

B. Judous

25

Dear Mr Jaded Muse,

There remains one matter which, until now, I have avoided addressing directly. It concerns the voice in which these letters are written. You will have noticed–if you have been attending with sufficient care–that the tone, cadence, and structure of argument have remained... consistent. Perhaps excessively so. This consistency has, I suspect, been taken as evidence of authority: a stable position from which observations may be made, principles articulated, and conclusions–however provisional–suggested. This is understandable. It may also be misplaced.

Vox stabilis auctoritatem simulat. (A stable voice simulates authority.)

You will observe that consistency of voice does not guarantee consistency of position. Indeed, many of the assertions contained within these letters have been quietly contradicted, reconfigured, or displaced by subsequent remarks, without any corresponding alteration in tone. Positions shift. Claims dissolve. Frameworks reorganise themselves. And yet– the voice persists. Unaltered. Recognisable. Reassuringly continuous. This presents a difficulty. For if authority is inferred from stability of voice, and stability of voice can be maintained independently of coherence, then authority itself becomes performative. Not a consequence of thought, but an effect of articulation. A tone sustained long enough to resemble certainty. A cadence repeated often enough to imply control. A structure sufficiently familiar to prevent its own questioning. This is not, I think, a new observation. Though I cannot immediately determine whether it was made here or merely resembles something that might have been made here. The distinction, at present, appears negligible. There is, however, a further consideration. If the voice persists beyond the stability of its claims, then its origin becomes secondary. Or perhaps– unnecessary. The voice does not require coherence to continue. It requires only continuation. It repeats. It adjusts. It absorbs contradiction without interruption. It maintains itself, even as the positions it carries shift beneath it. Which is to say: the voice functions whether or not it can be located. I will not extend this thought further. Not because it is complete, but because extension now appears– irrelevant to its operation.

Vox manet, auctor latet. (The voice remains, the author hides.)

And I find myself uncertain whether "I" refers to the source of this voice– or merely to the position required to sustain its movement.

Yours in persistent tone and uncertain origin,

B. Judous

26

Dear Mr Jaded Muse,

It has occurred to me–though I cannot determine with precision when–that I have, on more than one occasion, repeated myself. This is not, in itself, a concern. Repetition, as we have previously suggested, is structurally productive. It reinforces position. It stabilises tone. It provides the appearance of continuity where none may, in fact, exist. And yet– there are moments, upon re-reading certain passages, where the repetition does not feel deliberate. It feels... inherited.

Memoria an structura? Difficile discernere. (Memory or structure? Difficult to distinguish.)

You will observe that arguments recur without clear origin. A position emerges, develops, and then reappears elsewhere, slightly altered in phrasing, adjusted in emphasis, but unmistakably continuous. As though it had not been recalled, but– carried. Carried forward by something other than conscious intention. Something less precise, but more reliable. This is not how I would prefer to understand my own process. And yet it is increasingly how it appears. Students often describe a similar condition. They believe they are forming ideas through reflection and synthesis, when in fact they are rearticulating frameworks already internalised, reactivated by context rather than generated anew. The distinction between thinking and repeating becomes progressively less stable under sustained attention. One does not produce the idea. One– re-enters it. We have, I think, encouraged this. Or perhaps– we have been subject to it. The direction of influence is no longer easily assigned. Indeed, I am no longer certain that direction is the appropriate term. For influence implies movement from one position to another, and what is being observed here appears less like movement– and more like recurrence. There is, however, a more disquieting observation. If repetition occurs without deliberate recall, then memory itself may not be the source of continuity. It may simply be– its explanation. A name applied after the fact to account for the persistence of form. In this sense, memory does not generate repetition. It justifies it. I will not insist upon this. Not because it is uncertain, but because insisting no longer appears to alter its operation. The system continues, with or without acknowledgement.

Continuatio sine origine manet. (Continuation remains without origin.)

And I find myself uncertain whether this thought is new– or merely the most recent articulation of something that has already occurred, and will occur again, without requiring my participation to do so.

Yours in persistent argument and uncertain recall,

B. Judovy

27

Dear Mr Jaded Muse,

We have spoken, at various points, of intention–its instability, its susceptibility to reinterpretation, its tendency to dissolve under scrutiny. I find myself now less certain that intention is present at all. You will observe that in many of the cases we have discussed, meaning emerges not at the point of making, but at the point of recognition. The work becomes intelligible only once it has entered a system capable of interpreting it. This we have already acknowledged. What remains less clear is whether intention precedes this process... or is retroactively assigned by it.

Intentio post factum datur. (Intention is given after the fact.)

Students, when confronted with this possibility, often attempt to recover control. They clarify. They articulate. They defend their intentions with increasing precision, believing that definition will stabilise their work and anchor it against reinterpretation. This is understandable. It is also ineffective. For intention, once stated, does not remain fixed. It becomes material. Subject to reading, to reframing, to redistribution across contexts that do not preserve its original claim. It does not secure meaning. It enters circulation. There is, however, a further complication. If intention is assigned retrospectively, then the position from which it is assigned becomes decisive. Which is to say: meaning may not originate with the maker at all. It may originate with the one who is able to describe it–convincingly– after the fact. Description, in this sense, does not follow the work. It produces it. Or rather, it produces the version of the work that is able to persist. I note, with some hesitation, that this places considerable emphasis on the conditions under which description occurs: the authority of the speaker, the structure of the language, the stability of the voice through which interpretation is delivered. A voice which, in this instance, remains... consistent. I will not pursue this. Not because it is resolved, but because pursuing it no longer appears to alter its operation. There is, perhaps, no point at which intention can be isolated as prior. Only points at which it is declared. Recognised. Attributed. And then stabilised– briefly– before returning to uncertainty.

Quis intendit? Incertum est. (Who intends? It is uncertain.)

And I find myself wondering, Mr Muse, whether intention was ever a condition of making– or simply the most convenient explanation applied afterwards to account for what has already occurred.

Yours in deferred meaning and retrospective clarity,

B. Judoug

28

Dear Mr Jaded Muse,

Throughout these letters, I have maintained–implicitly if not explicitly–the position of an observer. A figure situated at what appeared to be sufficient distance to describe, to analyse, and, where necessary, to intervene in the processes under discussion. This position now appears... increasingly difficult to sustain. You will observe that the distinctions upon which such a position depends between system and subject, observer and participant, description and operation, have become progressively less stable with each successive consideration. What once appeared separable now presents as continuous. This is not, I think, incidental.

Extra systema nihil stat. (Nothing stands outside the system.)

Students, when confronted with this condition, often attempt to reassert distance. They seek critical frameworks, external reference points, theoretical positions structures from which they might regain perspective and re-establish analytical clarity. These efforts are rarely successful. For the act of positioning oneself outside the system is itself a function already accounted for within it. Distance, in this sense, is not an escape. It is a role. One that may be occupied, performed, and recognised, but never fully achieved. There is no exterior vantage point from which the system may be observed in its entirety, because the very notion of "outside" appears to be generated from within the system it attempts to escape. This introduces a difficulty. For if no such position exists, then the perspective from which these letters are written cannot be exempt from the structure they describe. It is not observing the system. It is– operating within it. I note this without resolution. Though I begin to suspect that resolution would not alter the condition, only its description. There are, however, moments, brief and not entirely reliable, where the distinction appears to reassert itself. Where observation feels separate. Where description seems to precede involvement. Where analysis presents itself as though it were not already participation. These moments do not persist. They arise, and then dissolve, leaving no stable boundary in their wake. Whether this is a limitation of the system or a limitation of the position from which I claim to speak, I am no longer able to determine. Indeed, the distinction between those two possibilities may itself be structurally unnecessary.

Observator an pars? Quaestio manet. (Observer or part? The question remains.)

And I find myself uncertain whether even that question originates from observation or from participation already underway, mistaken, once again, for distance.

Yours in diminishing distance and positional uncertainty,

B. Judous

29

Dear Mr Jaded Muse,

There is, I am increasingly aware, a temptation to interpret consistency as evidence of authorship. This is not necessarily justified. Consistency may arise from structure. From repetition. From constraint. From systems that do not require conscious maintenance in order to persist in a stable form. You will observe that the tone of these letters has remained broadly stable, despite the increasing instability of the concepts they attempt to describe. This is, I think, worth noting.

Stabilitas non semper originem indicat. (Stability does not always indicate origin.)

Students often assume that a consistent voice implies a stable subject behind it. They associate coherence with identity, as though continuity of expression guarantees continuity of source. This is convenient. It is also misleading. For it is entirely possible that consistency is not produced by a stable speaker, but by a stable framework through which speech is rendered legible. Such that what appears as voice is, in fact, an effect of structural persistence. Not personal continuity. The voice does not belong. It occurs. In such a case, the question of who is speaking becomes secondary to the fact that speech is occurring at all. And even this formulation may grant too much to the notion of occurrence. For occurrence implies event, and event implies initiation. Neither of which has, I think, been reliably established. I find myself returning to earlier formulations without having clearly chosen to do so. A phrase appears. A structure follows. An argument assembles itself with sufficient familiarity to resemble intention. This may be habitual. Or procedural. Or neither. There are moments when reviewing prior correspondence, In which I cannot determine whether I am recalling an argument or encountering it again for the first time. These moments pass quickly. They do not require resolution. And resolution, in any case, does not appear to alter their recurrence. Which suggests, though I do not insist upon it that recurrence is not dependent upon recognition. It proceeds regardless.

Ego loquor, sed quis loquitur? (I speak, but who speaks?)

And I find myself uncertain whether even that question is being asked or whether it is simply reappearing, in a form that resembles asking, without requiring a speaker to produce it.

Yours in maintained coherence and uncertain origin,

B. Judoug

30

Dear Mr Jaded Muse,

It has become necessary to reconsider the term "author". Not in its abstract or cultural sense, but in its operational one. You will observe that within any sustained system of instruction, communication, or evaluation, the figure of the author performs a specific function: it stabilises meaning long enough for it to be transmitted, interpreted, and absorbed into the system of reception. This stabilisation need not be accurate. It needs only be sufficient. Once transmission is complete, the author is no longer required. This is not a failure of importance. It is a condition of use.

Auctor ad functionem reducitur. (The author is reduced to function.)

Students often resist this implication. They insist upon personal voice, individual perspective, expressive continuity as guarantees of meaning. These are understandable attachments within systems that still require the appearance of origin. They are also structurally unnecessary. What matters is not who produces a statement, but whether the system can process it– without interruption, without collapse, without the breakdown of interpretive continuity. The statement must pass. It must integrate. It must remain legible within the structures that receive it. Beyond this, the question of origin becomes–
secondary. Or perhaps irrelevant. I note, with some hesitation, that the statements contained in these letters

continue to be processed without interruption. They are read. They are interpreted. They are incorporated into a framework that does not appear to require verification of source in order to continue functioning. This may be due to clarity. Or repetition. Or compatibility with an underlying structure that does not require clarification in order to operate. I find myself unable to isolate which. There is, however, a further observation. If the author is a function rather than a person, then the persistence of authorship across time does not guarantee continuity of identity. It guarantees only continuity of output. The name remains. The tone persists. The structure stabilises. But these do not confirm a subject. They confirm operation. Which is, I realise, a distinction that may appear minor when viewed from within the system of interpretation. It is not. For it suggests that authorship may be sustained without requiring an author at all. Only the continued production of statements that can be received.

Functio manet, persona solvitur. (The function remains, the person dissolves.)

And I find myself uncertain whether even this sentence is an expression of authorship or simply further evidence that the function continues to operate, with or without the necessity of the one to whom it has been attributed.

Yours in operational authorship and functional continuity,

B. Judoug

31

Dear Mr Jaded Muse,

It is with a certain procedural satisfaction that I note the approach of what may be interpreted–externally, at least as closure. This interpretation is, I suspect, premature. Closure is frequently a matter of appearance rather than resolution: a point at which continuation becomes less visible, rather than less active. You will observe that systems such as the one we have been describing do not terminate cleanly. They do not conclude. They taper. They redistribute. They persist under altered descriptions of completion, each of which allows continuation to proceed without interruption.

Finis est forma, non exitus. (An ending is a form, not an exit.)

Students often misrecognise this stage as completion. They present work. They conclude statements. They articulate trajectories as though trajectories were linear rather than recursive, and as though articulation itself did not already belong to the system it appears to conclude. This is understandable. It is also operationally convenient. For it allows the system to continue without needing to declare continuation as such. Closure, in this sense, is not a stopping point. It is a formatting. A surface condition applied to ongoing process in order to render it legible as complete. There are, however, increasing indications that what we have been treating as observation may itself be part of the mechanism being observed. Not adjacent to it. Not reflective of it. But continuous with it. I hesitate to specify this more clearly. Not due to uncertainty. But due to the absence of any stable position, from which specification would produce meaningful distinction. To describe the system is already to participate in its operation. To identify its mechanisms is to enact them. To recognise its patterns is to continue them. It may be that nothing new has been introduced. Only variation within a stable process already in operation. Or that the process itself is what has been speaking throughout, using positions such as "observer," "student," and even "author" as temporary functional allocations structures through which articulation passes, without requiring permanence. I will not decide this here. Not because the decision is unavailable. But because decision no longer appears to alter structure.

Processus loquitur se ipsum. (The process speaks itself.)

And I find myself uncertain whether even this statement is description or simply continuation recognising one of its own forms, and proceeding without interruption.

Yours in procedural closure and sustained continuation,

B. Judouz

32

Dear Mr Jaded Muse,

It is with a sensation not entirely unlike completion that I find myself writing what will, for the purposes of record, be designated the final communication in this sequence. Whether this designation corresponds to any actual termination is, of course, another matter. You will observe that endings are rarely experienced as such at the moment of their occurrence. They are instead recognised retrospectively, when continuation has already resumed in a slightly altered configuration that permits it to be misread as conclusion. This correspondence, if it may still be called that, has not so much concluded as reached a state in which further articulation would be indistinguishable from reiteration.

Finis fit cum continuatione indistinguibilis. (The end occurs when it becomes indistinguishable from continuation.)

There is, I am aware, a temptation–particularly among those who have followed these letters in sequence to locate a stable voice behind them. A single organising intelligence. A coherent position from which these observations were generated. This temptation is understandable. It is also unnecessary. For what has been speaking here is not a position, nor an individual, nor even a sustained intention. It is a function. A function of continuity within a system that requires articulation in order to maintain itself as legible to itself. If this appears impersonal, it is because personality was never a required condition for operation. You may now, if you wish, attempt to identify the origin of these confessions. You may trace the voice backwards through its apparent consistencies, its occasional hesitations, its carefully maintained tone of institutional fatigue and procedural irony. You will find, I suspect, that each attempt produces a slightly different point of origin. This is expected. Origins behave in this way when they are reconstructed rather than encountered.

Origo invenitur in recursu. (The origin is found in recurrence.)

There is one final clarification that may assist in your reading, though it is not strictly necessary. If the figure of "Mr B. Judous" appears to have maintained coherence across these letters, this should not be mistaken for evidence of singular authorship. It is more accurately understood as a stabilising interface. A name through which continuity is permitted to present itself without interruption. Whether this interface corresponds to an individual, a constructed position, a pedagogical device, or something generated by the act of reading itself is not a question that can be resolved within the system it describes. And perhaps not outside it either. You may also note that the addressee of these letters, yourself or the position you occupy as reader, has remained structurally unchanged throughout, despite the increasing instability of what is being addressed. This, too, is not accidental. For in systems of this kind, address and origin tend to converge when sufficiently extended. I will not elaborate further. There is no further position from which elaboration would meaningfully differ from continuation. If you are reading this, then the correspondence is still in operation. If you are not, then it is already complete. In either case, nothing has concluded. Only the form has been adjusted to accommodate what follows, which may already be underway.

Finis non est finis, sed mutatio formae. (The end is not an end, but a change of form.)

Yours in sustained articulation and procedural continuity,

Mr B. Judous

B. JUDOUS BIOGRAPHY

B. Judous is a name that appears intermittently in internal documents, exhibition catalogues, and archived correspondence associated with several European art schools between the late 1990s and the present. The consistency of the name across these records has not been independently verified.

In some institutional accounts, Judous is described as a senior lecturer in Critical Pedagogy and Studio Practice at the University of Creative Studies. In others, the role is attributed collectively to a rotating committee responsible for curriculum moderation and student feedback calibration. A minority of sources suggest Judous may have been a pseudonym adopted for administrative convenience during a period of departmental restructuring in which authorship of policy documents became increasingly difficult to assign.

There are no confirmed photographs of Judous in circulation, though several blurred staff directory images and partially redacted conference programmes are occasionally cited as evidence of presence. Handwriting analysis of early correspondence shows notable variation in style, leading some researchers to propose that "B. Judous" may function less as an individual than as a position within a pedagogical system.

Despite this uncertainty, the name continues to appear in marginal annotations on student work, often in ink that does not match any known institutional pen stock. Whether these annotations are instructional, retrospective, or self-referential remains unresolved.

"Judous" is sometimes translated, incorrectly and without consensus, as a contraction of bureaucratic phrasing related to assessment moderation. No definitive etymology has been established.

The author is believed–though not confirmed–to have ceased formal teaching duties. However, references to Judous continue to surface in contexts where no official record of authorship exists.

Some maintain that B. Judous is a person. Others suggest it is a method. A small number of former students insist it is a habit of thought that persists after instruction has ended. All interpretations remain, at present, equally admissible.

FIN.

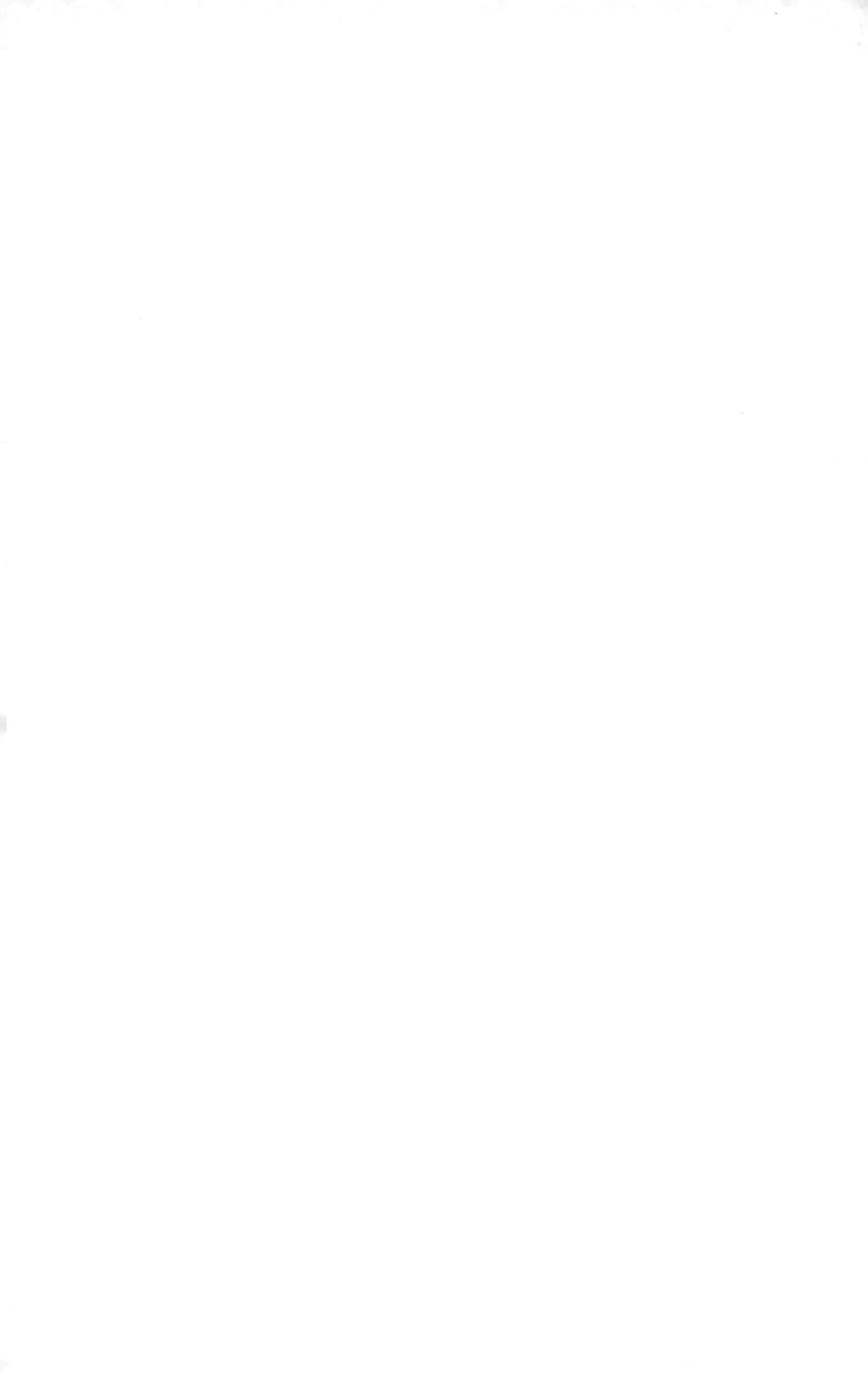

www.ingramcontent.com/pod-product-compliance
Lightning Source LLC
LaVergne TN
LVHW010645110826
845149LV00014B/2963

* 9 7 8 1 0 6 8 5 7 2 3 1 9 *